How to
CREATE YOUR OWN
Heaven on Earth

"A Spirit-Centered Journey
for
Everyday Living"

Ernest D. Martin

Copyright © 2019 by Ernest D Martin

All rights reserved.

No part of this book may be reproduced in any form or by any electronic or mechanical means, including information storage and retrieval systems, without written permission from the author, except for the use of brief quotations in a book review.

Print ISBN: 978-1-950036-06-6

eBook ISBN: 978-1-950036-07-3

DEDICATION

*This book is dedicated to my wife,
Denise Michaels, my love and lifetime partner.
Without her inspiration and involvement in
the book writing environment, this spiritual blog
would never have come to fruition as a book.*

*Thank you dear for your presence and interest
in my spiritual journey and your encouragement.
Thank you for putting up with me while I was often
working late at night expressing and
writing my blogs, while you went to sleep.*

CONTENTS

Foreword ix
Acknowledgments xi
Introduction xiii

Part I
GOD - THE DIVINE SPIRIT
1. Where Are You God? Are You There? 3
2. Are You Listening to Your Inner Voice? 5
3. Your Eyes-The Window to Your Soul 7
4. God's Power Is Free! Use It! 9
5. Things Will Happen in Their Own Divine Time 11
6. You Are On God's Schedule 13
7. God Is Your Partner 15
8. You Are On Divine Appointment 17
9. Interact And See God In Others 19
   God - The Divine Spirit ~ Prayer 21

Part II
LOVE IN ALL FORMS
10. God Loves You and the People Around You Back 25
11. Are Your Relationships Loving and Healthy? 27
12. Are You Afraid Of Loving Someone? 29
13. Love Heals 31
14. Share Spiritual Growth and the Love of God with Children 33
    Love in All Forms ~ Prayer 35

Part III
FAITH
15. Walk Your Own Path in Life 39
16. You are a Living Miracle 41
17. Tough Times are Temporary-Have Faith in God 43

18. Do You Think God is Testing You?	45
Faith ~ Prayer	47

Part IV
FREE WILL - DECISIONS

19. Walk the Talk	51
20. Take Action Now	53
21. Use God's Power and Shine	55
22. Choose to Release Negativity	57
Free Will Decisions - Prayer	59

Part V
PROSPERITY AND ABUNDANCE

23. Are You Bombarded by Materialism?	63
24. Prosperity is Yours for Asking	65
25. Find Balance in Our Material World	67
Prosperity and Abundance ~ Prayer	69

Part VI
RENEWAL AND THE POWER OF PRAYER

26. The Benefits of Prayer and Meditation	73
27. Listen to Others and Offer Prayers and Blessings	75
28. Your Prayers Get Results In Divine Time	77
Renewal and the Power of Prayer ~ Prayer	79

Part VII
JOY AND GRATITUDE

29. Praise God for Another Day	83
30. To Experience Joy, Serve Others	85
31. Teach Children God Loves All People	87
Joy and Gratitude ~ Prayer	89

Part VIII
BLESSINGS

32. Your Life has a Purpose	93
33. We Have Blessings and Lessons in Life	95
34. Give Thanks to God for Your Family, Friends and Prosperity	97

35. Angels Among Us	99
Blessings ~ Prayer	101

Part IX
HAPPINESS

36. Heaven on Earth Right Now	105
37. Allow Life to Flourish with Happiness and Joy	107
38. We Live in a Spiritual World Buffeted by the Physical World	109
39. Smile! You are Vibrating	112
Happiness ~ Prayer	115

Part X
PEACE AND HARMONY

40. Say "I am Peaceful and Harmonious" When Stressed	119
41. Let Go and Let God	121
42. You are not Going to Hell	123
Peace and Harmony ~ Prayer	125

Part XI
FORGIVENESS

43. Forgiveness is Great for the Soul	129
44. Have You Forgiven Yourself?	131
45. Release Those Old Grudges	133
46. How Diversity Taught Me Tolerance	135
Forgiveness ~ Prayer	137

Part XII
CARING AND SERVING

47. We are Ministers and Messengers	141
48. How Does God Use You to Serve Your Community?	143
49. Are Your Spiritual Beliefs Short on Action and Deed?	145
Caring and Serving ~ Prayer	147

Part XIII
YOUR PHYSICAL SELF

50. Is Your Body a Temple?	151
51. I Am Healthy And Prosperous	153

52. Accept Who You are as God Created You	156
Your Physical Self ~ Prayer	159
About the Author	161
Coming Soon	163

FOREWORD

Ernie is a highly dedicated minister, and author. He's committed to creating heaven on earth in his daily life. He always lives as a very happy man and is happy in his marriage to his wife Denise as well. Through his blogs he shares inspiration and renewal. He shows a genuine appreciation for life and its daily miracles. He believes life is miraculous and has lived an adventuresome life dedicated to love. Read this book. It will give you a renewed sense of joy and optimism. You won't regret it!

Robert Sidell
Attorney at Law
Author, "the Gateway"

ACKNOWLEDGMENTS

I am grateful to have grown up in an environment where various religions including Hindu, Muslim, Sikh, Buddhist and Christian were practiced. Growing up in Indian society, I learned tolerance as I gained an understanding of different belief systems. I managed to get along well with everyone while growing up.

I'm thankful for the numerous church-hopping journeys I took during the years I lived in Washington DC, the greater Los Angeles area and in Las Vegas. I'm grateful I found the Interfaith Council of Southern Nevada, where monthly discussions about a variety of religious topics energized my understanding and tolerance toward each participant. Through Interfaith, I attended the Parliament of the World's Religions convention, held in Salt Lake City, Utah in October 2015.

I am also grateful for a wonderful spiritual friend in Robert Sidell, Personal Injury Attorney and author of "The Gateway", and radio show host of "The Gateway" 840AM, KXNT, Las Vegas, on Sunday evenings. Robert invites me every week to offer a prayer at the end of his radio show. I've joined him many times on his Sunday afternoon prayer calls and for monthly meditations at his law office.

I am also thankful for a great friend, who is a devout Hindu, I met in 2014 at our local gym. He is Ajit Kundanani, an insurance agent and business owner. We work out together about four days a week, share God, faith and positive lifestyles as well as discuss international politics and culture. He always encouraged me when it came to writing this book.

My two grown sons, Steve and David, their families and my grandchildren have taught me plenty of patience, understanding, love and strengthened our family relationships. I'm hopeful my grandchildren will someday read this book.

My wife, Denise Michaels, author of, "Testosterone–Free Marketing," is a talented writer and book coach. She has played an important role in my life journey since 1997 when we met. She's been incredibly supportive about this book, and graciously took on the responsibility of editing it, sharing many ideas and tips along the way. Denise has gone to bed before me many nights so I could concentrate on writing. I seem to write well late at night. She's also been my sounding board and my constant support, I love you, dear.

Many thanks also to Hannah Kramer, and Audrey Moran for proofreading, to Kevin Vain for my book cover design and to Lisa Frederickson for the interior formatting and publishing of this book.

INTRODUCTION

The idea of writing a spiritual blog came to me in 2013. I wanted to share with readers how to live a life of peace, calm and limitless joy. A year earlier I anticipated writing about spiritual and religious festivals and celebrations with my social media friends. For some reason, it didn't come together as I wanted. Gradually my enthusiasm waned.

I considered my spiritual and religious upbringing during my formative years in India as a Christian in a nation of Hindus, living in a city of Muslims. As an adult, journeying and living in the USA, understanding spirituality was an abiding passion of mine.

Suddenly Spirit within told me to start writing a spiritual blog from the heart, based on my personal life experiences and circumstances. I finally was moved to share ways to discover and contribute to the well-being of our fellow man or woman; all a part of our community of humanity. After writing about 40 blogs, my wife Denise suggested, "Why don't you consider writing a book?"

INTRODUCTION

Since she's a Book Coach and a Ghostwriter, who's helped many people with their books over the years, I took her idea seriously.

I believe in writing based on my inner guidance, which for me comes from God. It also springs from my spiritual life journey. So, I decided to go for it. I wrote over one hundred spiritual blogs. As I wrote, I felt enthusiastic and happy about my decision. I loved the wonderful comments I received on many of the passages you're about to read. I'm grateful God gave me the patience and inspiration to move forward.

Once I was ready, I narrowed it down to the best writings, expressing how each of us can create Heaven for ourselves right here on Earth. These 52 short readings reflect God and Spirituality as I see and feel it from within. They also express how I believe it applies to everyday life. Some readers will go through the book quickly. However, I feel it's best enjoyed and absorbed by reading a chapter or blog each week. Then, take time to meditate, pray or ruminate on its message. Consider if it applies to you and your life. Within a year, you'll have read the entire book and have transformed yourself and your thoughts into a person who is happier, more peaceful and one who enjoys a deeper connection to Spirit.

Everything you'll read is based on my observations about how to live in happy, joyful, harmonious, compassionate, kind, gentle, prosperous, healthy, loving and spiritual ways every day of your life.

I've experienced family, raising children, great friends, good health, world travel and abundant prosperity. During my professional career I held jobs in the corporate world and positions working for non-profits. I've lived in multi-religious communities. I've volunteered and served. I've enjoyed intimate moments of love, quiet feelings of faith and devotion, prayer and meditation. All have shaped who I am and what you'll read on these pages.

INTRODUCTION

All are expressed and shared as moments in my spiritual journey and yours, too.

This book is about experiencing your own personal version of heaven right here on earth. It's about making this place a heavenly one for all who choose it. The core of this book is expressed as experiencing God from within as an action to create the life you want. God is and God is all there is. Spirituality is a way of life and an inner-directed awareness of the Divine Spirit within; to live a life that brings meaning and purpose.

There is a greater power and force than all of us united which is infinite, unseen and immortal. I believe God resides in each one of us and you're made in the image of God.

We are all ministers and messengers in our own unique way. You are here on planet Earth to help and learn life lessons from others. You are blessed with free will and can make the choice to live a joyful, happy, loving and kind-hearted life. Or not.

I purposely wrote these 52 essays to minimize negativity, judgment, condemnation, egotism, self-centeredness, greed, lack, and to encourage love, caring, excellent health, sharing, forgiveness, gratitude and thankfulness. When combined with your personal practice of prayer or meditation, helping others, tolerance for those who are different, faith in God and living your divine appointment, you can enjoy a new level of happiness and contentment no matter what's happening in the outside world. You'll have the grace and power to move forward from a place of divine guidance and God centeredness. You can authentically express God from within in a way no one else can because it's unique to you.

You'll notice there is no mention of any specific religion or tradition. You'll find no mention of prophets, past and present messengers, or any quotations or references from other religious books. Everything I share with you comes from God within expressing as

INTRODUCTION

Ernie. Spirit has a way of using each one conveyed almost magically through our talents and abilities. You can do it too when you simply listen to what comes to you from within, trust its message and communicate it to others in your own special way. God's blessings are everywhere because we're all spiritual beings, having a human experience.

You and I are incredibly fortunate and privileged to have this life, in this world, with rules, structure and order. Humanity has created culture for different nations and laws to minimize chaos and confusion for its citizens on this physical plane.

Give thanks and praise to God, the source of your being and enjoy your physical life in what can be Heaven on Earth.

It feels even more heavenly when you do your best to get along with your family, neighbors and friends within your community. Your mission in life is to love God and yourself. Share your love with others to make our earthly family a little better.

God's blessings to you. I hope you enjoy the book and share it with others.

PART I
GOD - THE DIVINE SPIRIT

WHERE ARE YOU GOD? ARE YOU THERE?

GOD - THE DIVINE SPIRIT

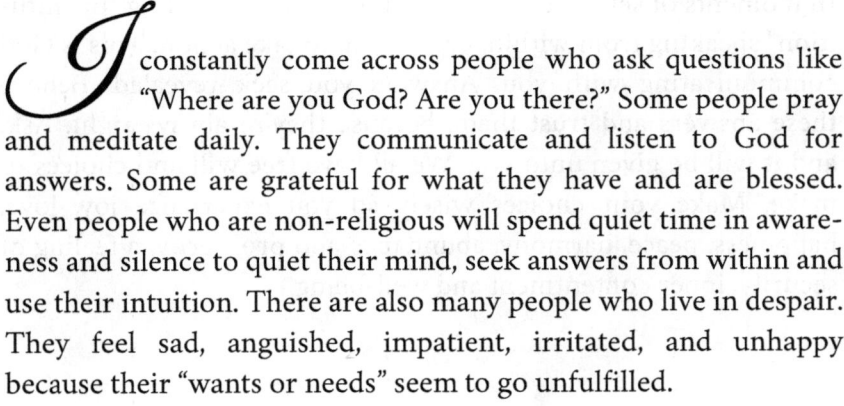

I constantly come across people who ask questions like "Where are you God? Are you there?" Some people pray and meditate daily. They communicate and listen to God for answers. Some are grateful for what they have and are blessed. Even people who are non-religious will spend quiet time in awareness and silence to quiet their mind, seek answers from within and use their intuition. There are also many people who live in despair. They feel sad, anguished, impatient, irritated, and unhappy because their "wants or needs" seem to go unfulfilled.

The challenge lies in experiencing the requests made. After prayer, do you move your feet into action? Have you started talking and sharing with others about what you desire? Have you prayed and meditated with faith, believing your good is already done for you?

Bring your intuition into alignment with what you desire and want to experience. Do you pray or meditate only when you have problems? Do you struggle with finances, debt, ill-health, faulty relationships and unhappiness? Many people turn to God and plead for help when things seem desperate and they don't know where else to turn.

Take it from me: You aren't likely to find the answers to your problems at the worship or lecture places where you find pastors or speakers who preach "instant feel good" remedies. The answers and solutions to your challenges are within. They can only be implemented through the pathway of action.

God reveals all answers and directions from within right where you're out. God Is. God is all there is. God surrounds you. God is within you. There is something greater than yourself which sustains your life, that's infinite and unseen. Some people call this presence God, Lord, Almighty, Force, Energy and the Universe.

In moments of self-awareness you'll notice a "gut feeling" or "intuition" speaking from within, urging you to take action. This is God communicating with you. Answers you seek revealed. Believe these answers and trust them, because they're always right. Ask, and it will be given unto you. We all have free will and choices to make. Make your choices wisely so you experience joy, love, happiness, peace, harmony, abundance and prosperity, a feeling of security, inner contentment and well-being.

ARE YOU LISTENING TO YOUR INNER VOICE?

GOD - THE DIVINE SPIRIT

We all trudge along in our everyday walk of life. You probably have wants, needs, desires and goals you want to achieve. You want joy, fulfillment, inner contentment, compassion, peace and harmony within yourself and others. You pray or meditate and ask God or the Infinite, Higher Power, Source, Lord, for financial prosperity, excellent health and great relationships. Soon you'll discover the answers are all within. They aren't "out there" somewhere. Are you open to listening from within? Are you listening to your vibrations, "your gut," your intuition? Do you trust your inner instincts, which are always God communicating to you?

From my own experiences, I sometimes let job opportunities, learning a new profession, even romantic relationships pass me by. I didn't always listen to my inner voice, but I kept moving doing the same old things or following the same routine with different expectations. Then, there came a time when I had to make a serious commitment to change. I decided to accept new opportunities and say "yes!" to what life offered. I went through a time of inner reflection via meditation and by talking to my small circle of trusted friends.

In a way, we must be ready to jump in or take risks to step in. I've witnessed singles in long-term relationships delaying marriage because they were waiting for the right partner to come along. Or, they questioned or doubted whether their relationships were the right ones. This boils down to developing a sense of inner trust and becoming clearer about what their heart and mind tells them. In these moments, it's a good idea to sit down in prayer and meditation and ask for God's guidance.

If you're unsure about the feedback you get regarding issues of concern, talk with a trusted friend or a couple friends. Make sure these friends are people who have a positive outlook on life. Talk with people who are confident and encouraging. But in the end remember, you're still the decision maker. Consider all the choices you have at your disposal. Prayer and meditation are a great relaxer and will help bring you inner harmony and answers.

So, listen from within. Listen to what your instincts and gut tell you about what you seek and desire to experience. Communicate to God via prayer and meditation. Be open for the answers revealed to you. Follow up on the clues as they're revealed to you. Try not to be wishy-washy regarding the answers you receive. Check everything out. The God who created the universe is loving and friendly, so you can pursue your journey for fulfillment, joy, compassion, love, kindness, peace and understanding.

YOUR EYES-THE WINDOW TO YOUR SOUL

GOD - THE DIVINE SPIRIT

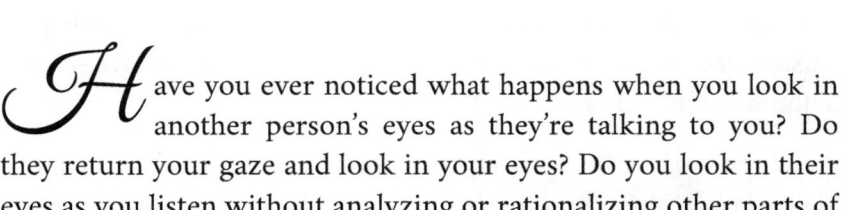

*H*ave you ever noticed what happens when you look in another person's eyes as they're talking to you? Do they return your gaze and look in your eyes? Do you look in their eyes as you listen without analyzing or rationalizing other parts of their body or personality?

Our eyes are the window to our soul. There is something special about our eyes. You can see yourself in another person's eyes and see straight into their mind and soul. They can see your soul through your eyes, too. The beautiful part is to be aware of this when you look into another person's eyes while sharing and talking. You'll see your spirit or God within you while looking deep in their eyes. This phenomena of connecting with the divine inside each other subconsciously through our eyes in the moment we're connected will help you see the charm and beauty in each person you encounter.

As a minister and wedding officiant, I've seen many marrying couples standing just two feet away from me, exchanging their wedding vows and rings. I see in their eyes the joy, the love, elation, light, attraction and the closeness as they project into each other's eyes and into their souls. Most brides are deeply emotional and teary-eyed at this moment. I've seen several grooms shed tears, too. I ask the couple to hold hands and look into each other's eyes as they repeat their wedding vows. The couple shows God within each of them in action within each other's soul. I feel so much joy and elation while looking in the couple's eyes, as they express their wedding promises and exchange rings.

So, next time you meet someone new, make an effort to make eye contact. Maybe it's an encounter as simple as at a grocery store when the cashier looks at you as you pay for your groceries. Look into his or her eyes. See yourself in their eyes and allow them to see their divine self in your eyes. Do this next time you see and converse with a supervisor at work, your business associates, your customers, when you're at school/college, your minister at a church/temple, or a server at a restaurant.

You'll be amazed how much trust and confidence you'll instantly develop with people. Looking into people's eyes with focus also helps the other person. They'll develop trust and confidence in you, too. Let the God in you shine forth.

GOD'S POWER IS FREE! USE IT!

GOD - THE DIVINE SPIRIT

*E*lectricity at home, a business, a coffee shop or even at a place of worship costs money. But God's power is free to use every day. Recognize it and be aware of it.

It's right where you are; inside you and surrounding you. You don't have to attend a church, a temple or other holy place to connect with God. Sure, you can attend worship services to gain a sense of community with other members and friends as you participate and listen to the ceremony and prayers. But God resides inside you and me all the time. Recognize and be fully aware of the Creator's power within. Use it for your loving relationships, your health, prosperity, forgiveness and for serving others.

During my thirties and early forties I went "church hopping" to find spirituality, God and even love in my personal life. I thought God was "out there." My fellow seekers became friends as well. We were in the same boat looking for God and some relief from the day-to-day hustle bustle. Personally, I was dependent on "other ministries and churches" instead of acknowledging God and spirit within me. Using God's power from within combined with positive affirmations does wonders. Say these affirmations to yourself:

- I am prosperous;
- I am healthy;
- I am attracting love in my life;
- I am forgiving and I forgive myself;

And so on. The "I am" is a way of using God's power and it's free.

Next time when you're walking around a shopping center, supermarket, place of worship, or where you work; look for God in others. Isn't it wonderful to see Spirit in action in each person you meet? We're all blessed with free will and choices. Your decisions have consequences and will determine your life experience. The more you think about God's love in your daily life, the better you're likely to feel about yourself and you'll treat others more lovingly. So, use God's power inside you. There's no charge, but the benefits are priceless. All that's necessary is your desire and the will to turn it on and apply God's power.

THINGS WILL HAPPEN IN THEIR OWN DIVINE TIME

GOD - THE DIVINE SPIRIT

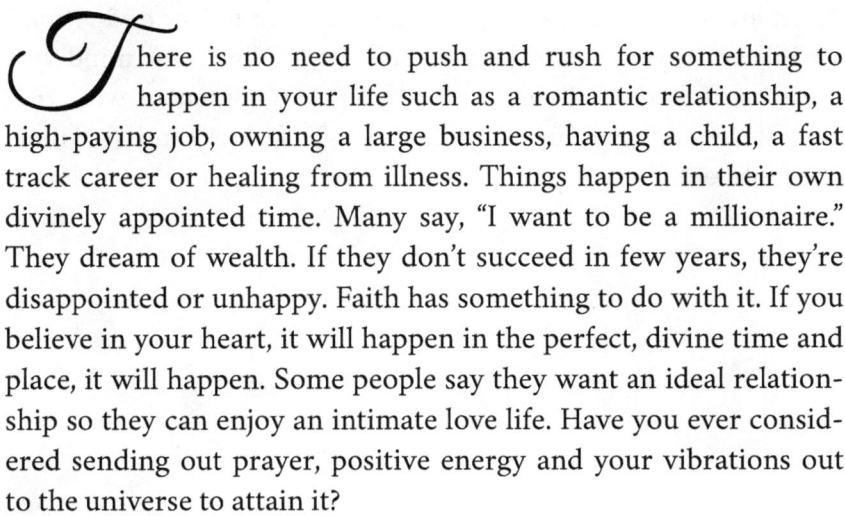

There is no need to push and rush for something to happen in your life such as a romantic relationship, a high-paying job, owning a large business, having a child, a fast track career or healing from illness. Things happen in their own divinely appointed time. Many say, "I want to be a millionaire." They dream of wealth. If they don't succeed in few years, they're disappointed or unhappy. Faith has something to do with it. If you believe in your heart, it will happen in the perfect, divine time and place, it will happen. Some people say they want an ideal relationship so they can enjoy an intimate love life. Have you ever considered sending out prayer, positive energy and your vibrations out to the universe to attain it?

There is an order and time in this world. I recall after my graduation where I received a bachelor's degree in Business at age 28, I had high expectations of becoming a manufacturing plant General Manager of a medium size company in the Los Angeles area in five to seven years. In the mid-1970's, many steel and manufacturing companies were going through a transition phase in America.

They were shipping raw materials out to be manufactured and completed in Mexico or China. So, there were fewer opportunities for the position I sought. This reality resulted in me pursuing other job opportunities including manufacturing costing and project costing. This is what I call God's divine timing as He makes it happen.

So, control your ego in the physical world by using your God-given free will to create good. We all have choices to make and then we take action.

Allow divine right timing to flow without forcing it. The same thing is true when it comes to forming close love relationships, or healing from sickness. Yes, pray for physical healing. If you have a desire to be wealthy, take action and let God do the rest. Your spirit and ego can sometimes clash. It's best to follow divine spirit and listen to your heart. Take a moment to align your mind with your heart, body and spirit. When you're in alignment with your divinity, things fall in place and you'll feel a sense of inner contentment.

YOU ARE ON GOD'S SCHEDULE

GOD - THE DIVINE SPIRIT

*H*ave you ever noticed how we go through life in this human experience? Most people long to enjoy a prosperous, loving, healthy life with lots of great experiences. Or, do you want to build a successful career or business? Having such aspirations and dreams is a wonderful thing. In fact, many of those dreams and aspirations may come to fruition for you. However, understand you're a spirit a human body for a finite time on earth. God has created you and you're on His schedule as you live in this world. No one truly knows when they'll leave this earth. God has a plan for each one of us and our lives. We're endowed and blessed with free will and have choices to make the world a better place to live in as we love each other.

Recently a friend of mine made his transition and is no longer on this earthly plane. He was ill for a long period. I visited him twice at his home and while he was in the hospital. I prayed with him each time. He was a devotional man and he praised God for keeping him alive and for allowing him to help others in the areas of health and well-being. Even though he faced pain and underwent medical treatments, he still wanted to provide information to help the elderly care for themselves. He also helped people who were ill or who had disabilities. He was an eloquent fellow and his hugs were always heartfelt. His way of serving God was through the personal testimony of his life experience and through sharing information about health and safety. God had a plan for Bob.

Our physical lives tend to be guided by our ego. Our peers including family members influence us in the direction of acquiring abundance or wealth, in the form of money. This can result in going astray in our loving relationships, or becoming addicted to endless hours of work. Look deep in your heart and ask whose plan you're on. When you can acknowledge you're on God's plan, you'll surely see the light which shines from within and reaches out to others to help them when they're in need or facing challenges. Be good to yourself, and you'll be good to others.

GOD IS YOUR PARTNER

GOD - THE DIVINE SPIRIT

*D*on't look up to the sky to find God. God is right where you are and in your heart. God Is. God is all there is. Surely God is bigger than the world we live in. God is energy, a vibration, powerful, infinite, an infinite spirit, a divine spirit and all-encompassing. All throughout your younger years and your adult life, you probably came to believe God was "out there" somewhere. Many people actually fear God. Why would anyone choose to fear God? God is love. Reasonable questions often asked include: "How can I reach out to God for help and support? Does He listen? Is He with me? Does He love me?" Yes, God loves you.

Experiment with this or check it out for yourself: Go to a loved one and say, "I am with you." Or say, "You and I are on the same wavelength." Or, "I know you care about me." There is no fear in expressing this dialogue, right?

Now, in your prayer and meditation or when conversing with God, talk to God in the same way as you talked to your loved one or a loving friend. See and feel the difference. God won't harm you or bite you. You're made in the image of God. You've been blessed with free will and choices to make during your lifetime. When you treat God as your partner rather than a distant, scary authority "up there," you'll feel a greater connection when it comes to expressing your love from within.

Your connection to God springs from how you view and believe in God within. God is greater than each of us, keeping us alive and guiding us as we live our lives.

Team up with God as your partner and see how your personality is transformed. Many loved ones and friends will see the God within you in action. Then, they'll decide to partner with God as well. When you consider God as your partner, rather than fearing him, you're bound to enlighten yourself and, the love of God will pour within you. In this way you can help others and prosper in happiness, joy, financial prosperity and excellent health.

YOU ARE ON DIVINE APPOINTMENT

GOD - THE DIVINE SPIRIT

Have you ever tried to force things to happen? Like expecting a job interview, a promotion, or a sale in business? Perhaps it was initiating a relationship, completing higher education, wanting to lose weight or fighting biological clock to have children? Here is the good news: If your desire and faith are focused and you believe in yourself, followed by taking action, you're bound to bring these things to fruition. You'll enjoy the results of your efforts.

Have you ever noticed yourself going through life wondering why things aren't happening and clicking for you? The divine appointment must take place. Your intuition and God's grace makes it happen. Of course, prayer and meditation help as well.

In my professional corporate career as a Financial Analyst, I sent out resumes for jobs, especially during periods of high unemployment in the Aerospace and High-Tech industry. I often felt extremely confident I'd get a call for an interview and eventually I was hired. Positive thought created a positive result. But, was there a divine appointment? Was the job a good fit and was I qualified for it? My ego for the potential job was set high with expectations, but, I didn't always take the idea of a Divine Appointment into consideration. After a few months, a recruiter from the company or employment agency would call to ask if I was still available for a job opportunity.

While I was divorced, I hoped and expected a "perfect love" to come into my life. Of course, my love for a relationship (now my wife, Denise) was the result of a divine appointment. I admit, before then I went through numerous "coffee dates" with lovely ladies. I learned to not force myself into something which wasn't a divine appointment. Grace must come in its own right timing. Divine Spirit is already there. It needs to click with your intuition and be felt from the heart.

INTERACT AND SEE GOD IN OTHERS

GOD - THE DIVINE SPIRIT

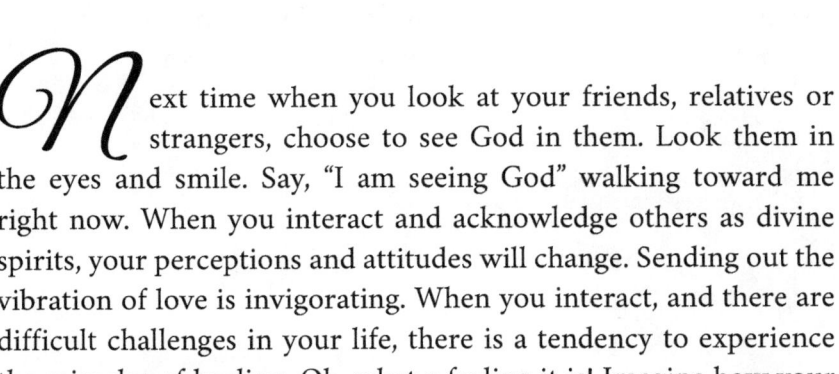

Next time when you look at your friends, relatives or strangers, choose to see God in them. Look them in the eyes and smile. Say, "I am seeing God" walking toward me right now. When you interact and acknowledge others as divine spirits, your perceptions and attitudes will change. Sending out the vibration of love is invigorating. When you interact, and there are difficult challenges in your life, there is a tendency to experience the miracles of healing. Oh, what a feeling it is! Imagine how your community, our nation and our world would be better if you acknowledged in each person the experience of God within. Feelings of hate, animosity, fear and mistrust would simply disappear. Love, trust, compassion and prosperity consciousness would awaken and grow.

I remember several times as I drove into the city and came across homeless people asking for money or food. I usually carry the phone number of the local rescue mission in our city, who serves a free dinner for the hungry. I try my best to give the homeless people I encounter the phone number to call the rescue mission. In many parts of America, there are non-profit agencies that will respond to a phone call from a homeless person, pick them up and drive them to the rescue mission. Help for the needy is available at no cost to the person seeking assistance. Sometimes, I feel God shows up in simple disguise in front of me seeking help.

We're all made in God's image. We all have a human face to fulfill God's plan in this world. We're all a miracle. We learn and grow from our society's culture to obey our parents and authorities, and to make a living working for others or as a business owner.

See God at work, in your business, in your school, in your loved ones and in strangers, wherever you go. God is love. So, when you're in tune with God within and the wholeness of self, your defenses are likely to be lower and you'll experience harmony and peace. You're here to build your own heaven on earth.

GOD - THE DIVINE SPIRIT ~ PRAYER

Dear Lord,
Thank you for this blessed day.
Guide me to trust my inner voice,
so I can confidently make decisions
and choices in my everyday life.

I'm grateful, thankful and appreciative for
all the attributes of love, compassion,
giving, and human interaction
which you've instilled in me.

These attributes you've given all human
beings to apply, so we can take
positive action, living life fully.
Help me to see God in others, and see
the good in others creating heaven on earth.

So it is!

PART II
LOVE IN ALL FORMS

GOD LOVES YOU AND THE PEOPLE AROUND YOU BACK

LOVE IN ALL FORMS

Many times, we keep asking the question, "Who loves me?" Our craving of the heart seeks fulfillment. When I was single, I silently asked myself similar questions. Deep down, I knew my parents and siblings loved me. But many people overlook the fact that God loves us all; regardless of who you are.

God is always good. God always resides within you and you're surrounded with people who also have God within. They're God's people. Love is something you feel and accept. You know it when you feel touched from within. When you're open to the love of Divine Spirit, which is God, you're blessed with love, security and stability. Our human ego can be deceptive, so clear it from your heart and mind. Then you can recognize and receive love in your heart.

God, Higher Power or Spirit resides in each person regardless of their circumstances. Open your heart and mind to receive love from others. By acknowledging others and their willingness to spread love, you can embrace love. People close to you, whether they're loved ones, friends or even strangers, will open their hearts when you open yours. This opening must happen for love to flourish. As you dive into knowing yourself and examine how you treat yourself, your mindset makes it possible. If you constantly criticize and beat yourself up with unpleasant feelings, it's impossible to project happy thoughts or send positive vibrations outside your boundaries.

To receive love, discover how to pave the way for receiving. Your heart and mind must be ready and open to accepting others. Offer a smile and be pleasant to others. Go out of your way to assist people in need. When you build those habits from the inside, the Spirit of God within will attract others. In turn an environment is created where you can receive love from others.

You may wonder why you don't always experience love. Now you know what you must do to attract it into your life; project love and kindness from within toward people around you. See God in others as you witness and feel love returned to you. Love goes around.

ARE YOUR RELATIONSHIPS LOVING AND HEALTHY?

LOVE IN ALL FORMS

I believe without trust, commitment and love every day, our personal relationships with our significant other will go nowhere. The relationship will flounder and you won't experience joy or happiness. Instead you'll probably live with pain, longing and agony.

When you ask Divine Spirit or God to guide you in improving your love relationship, and make changes and adjustments, you're on a loving journey. Even our relationships with children must be genuine. Children can sense the truth within you. There's no need to give kids lectures on love. As you give and show unconditional love with children, you'll receive love unconditionally in return.

We're bombarded with excessive commercialism telling us to show love by buying a car, expensive jewelry, a gold watch or designer clothing for the one we love. Materialism doesn't buy love. Love and true generosity comes from the heart. Caring in a loving way, listening and sharing with your spouse or partner and telling each other "I love you" daily goes a long way.

I make a habit of telling my wife Denise, "I love you" at least once a day. Also, we've made a habit to hug for at least 20 seconds during our day. Love must come freely from the heart, not like a programmed robot.

I have several friends who've asked me how they can improve their love relationships. I ask them, "Do you communicate openly? Are you listening to your inner voice, which is God communicating through you?" I also ask them, "Do you understand each other in a loving way? Do you have a comfortable 'give and take' so you can enjoy balance in your relationship?"

As a wedding officiant, I read poems during my ceremonies on heartfelt love and marriage. It's important for couples to be aware of how heartfelt loving words and actions can strengthen their relationship over time. Find answers to the problems in your relationship by compromising. Or, seek help from your clergy or from relationship counselors.

Many people experience their ego in the form of superiority and financial manipulation as a way to grab power in their personal relationships. This type of relationship doesn't come from Spirit within. God or Spirit communicates from the heart. When you're out of sync with spirit, your relationship will sour. Ego and defensiveness take over. If possible, pray with each other and communicate to clear the air. Say "I love you" often.

ARE YOU AFRAID OF LOVING SOMEONE?

LOVE IN ALL FORMS

When I was divorced and single for several years, I found it difficult to say "I love you" to a single woman. But, I was willing to go on dates. I felt conflicted on the inside, but I moved with my ego self from the outside to fulfill my social desires. After a few years the routine of dating and shallow relationships grew old. I sat down and did some inner reflecting on love, trust, commitment and what I truly wanted. When you realize God loves you unconditionally, what prevents you from loving a partner unconditionally? The answer lies within, and when you look for answers you'll find it's easy. It's wonderful to ask Spirit within for answers to your questions about love.

Go to a quiet place. Meditate, pray and communicate with God about your love life and your issues or fears around trust, commitment and connecting with a loving partner, lover, or spouse. Trust your inner instincts and have faith in your heart: Listen and discern what is communicated back to you? What is God saying? Many people tend to "talk it over" with personal friends. This isn't the best solution.

Sure, friends can sometimes help. But, your ultimate decision to move forward with love comes from the guidance you receive from within, from God who loves you unconditionally and wants the best for you. Consider writing down the answers you receive during prayer and meditation for your understanding and for taking action.

We all go through the journey of budding romance to seek love, be loved and offer love to others with one special person in our lives.

Remember to trust yourself and make a commitment to openness, to give love and be yourself in relationship. Pray and ask God for inner guidance, a wonderful love life, and eventually for marriage to tie the knot. God is right where you are, inside you. God is all over you. There is no need to go looking for God. So, get ready to meet your special love knowing Divine Spirit will guide you in your romantic adventure to give and receive love. Leave your judgements behind and expect the miracle of love to happen.

LOVE HEALS

LOVE IN ALL FORMS

There is so much happening in the world we live in. Constant political skirmishes in the Middle East. There are problems in countries where minorities aren't treated poorly. We also have problems with division and a lack of unity in America, which needs to be resolved.

God is Love. You were made in the image of God. Accept the fact that through your love from the heart, you touch others. When you acknowledge and are aware of God's love, you're in alignment and can share it with others. People have the capacity to give and share love when you accept it and acknowledge it for yourself.

Love should never be hoarded. It's meant to be shared with others. Imagine, when love is finally shared all over the world, we'll no longer have animosity or hatred toward others.

My observation of the Middle East, where things are both fluid and dangerous, due to inequality and ongoing struggles for power is that love becomes an illusion. It's only through faith in God and understanding our human conditions that we find peace and respect for others. Love has a way of conquering fear.

I'm highly optimistic that love always surrounds us. When I choose to see myself and people around me with love, I know my love touches and heal others. I've also discovered and recognized, love must be accepted and acknowledged by the heart. Without acknowledgment, love is received as an observation, rather than allowing yourself to be immersed in love.

You read about it and see it on TV; the suffering of minorities through religious persecution, through famine where people go to bed hungry or through homelessness in our own communities.

When you pray with love in your heart to heal your shortcomings, your vibrational waves touch the people you think about. This is where you can apply prayer and meditation to pray for the welfare of people who are less fortunate. Many times, people are influenced by their own devotion and faith. You can strengthen the cause for hope and healing for those who experience persecution, hunger or homelessness.

SHARE SPIRITUAL GROWTH AND THE LOVE OF GOD WITH CHILDREN

LOVE IN ALL FORMS

We're all children of God and made in God's image. I believe children should be taught about spirituality and God beginning at an early age. It's important to let them know God loves them and, God is always available right where they are--within themselves.

I have two grown sons. They were introduced to church through Catholicism early on, when they were in kindergarten. I'm a proponent of sharing spiritual growth from the perspective of a loving God rather than one based on fearing God. Many people were raised to fear God, as a central part of their faith. The truth is God loves us dearly. But love and fear contradict each other. When we share God's love with our children as they grow, they'll respect the divinity and Spirit within themselves.

God's blessings are enormous. Teach your children to pray for God's bounty and blessings. As a young boy, growing up in India, at age five or six, we always said a blessing or grace at our family meal.

Our simple prayer was, "God bless this food." That's it. That was our family prayer before eating dinner. When I started attending a boy's Christian boarding school in South India at the age of 12, we all prayed together as a group in the dining room before eating our meal. Regardless of your beliefs, teach your children to appreciate God's blessing in all walks of life.

Teach your children to love God. Combined with your own personal and spiritual growth, it will surely help your children develop and function well in their family, as well as in their community as a whole.

Love has no boundaries. Your children will be productive, do well in school, and become successful adults in their chosen profession, working for others or in their own business. It all starts with your own awareness of Divine Spirit and making your children aware. Combine this with spreading love. Imagine eliminating hate and discord as the years go by in our society. As we teach God and spirituality to our children, in the process, adults will learn and be more aware of God's love and presence in each of us.

LOVE IN ALL FORMS ~ PRAYER

Dear Lord,
Thank you for giving me this precious life.
Thank you for allowing me to experience this
adventurous journey of life.

I pray my love remains strong with
my loved ones, friends, others in my
community and around the world.
Whenever I face setbacks in my relationships
with my loved ones and friends, I will recognize it,
and make adjustments in my attitudes
and thoughts to strengthen my bonds.

I pray my relationships are loving and
healthy, creating heaven on earth.

And so it is!

PART III
FAITH

WALK YOUR OWN PATH IN LIFE

FAITH

*Y*our parents helped raise you throughout your childhood into adulthood. You were shown how your family worshipped and believed in a faith system palatable to their tradition and way of life. They taught you right from wrong and how to take responsibility for your actions.

Or you didn't grow up with parents, so you were raised by other relatives or in state institutions. Either way, when you finally become an adult, you're bombarded with a multitude of choices and decisions to make on your path through life. Your God-given free will and your ability to make decisions for everyday living becomes part of your life journey. A journey where only you are responsible for your actions. The Divine Spirit, God or Lord if you prefer, is always within.

Soon you begin to realize something is guiding you through your life journey. When I was younger, I recall constantly asking friends or even looking in books for "opinions, approval and judgement" every time I was faced with a decision with several choices before me. But, there's something in each of us, many people overlook—the inner spirit.

I'm referring to the Divine Spirit bestowed upon us by God. It's both unseen, and yet it speaks to us. Are you listening? It takes courage and guts to listen to your inner voice. Do you:

- Trust yourself?
- Believe in yourself?
- Have self-confidence?
- Believe in your higher self?

Questions like these pop up at times. When you're aware of Spirit communicating within, you're offered choices to make decisions. You're responsible for making those decisions for your good and the good of others.

It sounds simple, but, the inner awareness of Spirit communicating within can help you experience your best journey of life while remaining yourself.

To experience your own inner awareness, start with meditation and prayer. Look at and explore your inner self. You'll find what you're looking for within.

Did you know you can entertain yourself by telling yourself silly jokes? You can find joy and happiness within. You can simply be yourself. Go and discover your inner self, which is God communicating within you. Listen to your heart and then act.

YOU ARE A LIVING MIRACLE

FAITH

Give thanks and praise to God for the miracle of you. Your existence on earth is a gift to humanity. How you live your life to fulfill God's plan will determine how happy, joyful, kind-hearted, compassionate, loving and forgiving you are. A helping hand to help a neighbor or even a stranger is a miracle. Caring for others is a miracle. Caring for your own health is a miracle. Your spiritual journey on your own path with awareness and discovery is a miracle. It's all about awakening. As you question the meaning of life, its existence and what you're here for, your journey will continue.

I recall living and driving in Southern California, as well as in Las Vegas, Nevada. I've encountered several near misses, narrowly avoiding an accident. In some instances, it was by inches. What a miracle! The Divine guided me and protected me all along. Once, back in 1998, just a couple weeks before I was scheduled to leave for India, I was sitting in the left turn lane waiting to turn into the apartment complex where I lived. Another driver hit me from behind. Thank God I wasn't seriously hurt. I had a couple sessions with a chiropractor and then took off for a ten week pilgrimage to India. I know God protected me and kept me safe. It was a miracle. Unexpected things happen in our lives. And, the infinite love of God protects us.

How many times have you gone through your everyday walk of life and didn't recognize or notice the everyday miracles you encountered?

Sometimes people reach out to you. They offer a smile or lend a hand. Many are willing to help. They're motivated and driven by a desire which springs from the inside to reach out and offer help or goodwill. As a spiritual being experiencing this earthly existence, you probably encounter constant small miracles. There is no rational reason or explanation for miracles. They just happen. Have faith in miracles. God creates the energy which moves through each one of us to witness them.

TOUGH TIMES ARE TEMPORARY-
HAVE FAITH IN GOD

FAITH

In times such as recessions, high unemployment, business failures, marriage conflicts, higher education challenges, financial problems, addiction issues, and on and on, there are signs of temporary setback. In the midst of it all, you may suddenly remember God or pray to God when facing hardships. Religious places of worship are crowded with every seat filled during tough times, by people hoping their problems will miraculously be solved by Divine Intervention. Or, they trust a minister or rabbi will spell out the answers to their problems.

Most people are imprisoned by excessive materialism and a desire to acquire more, more and more. This belief necessitates adjustments along the way. People tend to forget our deeper awareness, such as the divinity of each person's inner self. It's easy to let creature comforts, excess or materialism take over the essence of our being, from the environment in which we live.

Over the years, I've experienced recessions, unemployment, broken marriages, broken love relationships, and financial problems. I recall back in the early 1980's, when I was laid off from a corporation as a Cost Engineer, my inner confidence plummeted. I decided to serve as a volunteer phone lay minister at a church ministry. I listened to people with incredibly challenging stories. By comparison my own temporary setbacks didn't seem so bad.

Experiencing a divorce during this time was not helpful. I lost a lot of confidence in my ability to have a successful relationship. For several years making a commitment in a relationship was a challenge. One thing saved me, my trust and faith in God. I often prayed and spent time in meditation.

God is always available to you in good times and in challenging ones. Prayer and meditation is always a good way to strengthen your inner self. Tough times show up in our lives, because adjustments and changes need to occur, so our lives can be managed and adjustments made to our inner and outer environment. Your belief in God is strengthened when you face short-term obstacles. When you pray you communicate with God so you can experience joy, love, peace and harmony.

Think about what a bargain God is in your life. The only cost in strengthening your inner core with the energy of God is your time and commitment. You have a direct link to God through prayer if you choose to access it. You're always in good hands with God.

DO YOU THINK GOD IS TESTING YOU?

FAITH

You go through life with a great family. You have a job, a career or a thriving business which provides income and status. One day, things begin to crumble. Your marriage or personal relationships are suddenly on the rocks or worse, they break up. Unemployment appears to be on the horizon and you begin to feel insecure like you might lose your job. Or, your business isn't cutting it. Sales have dropped and you're trying to decide if you should close the doors.

Is God testing you? No, No, No. God isn't testing you. God is love. God is light, always eternal and always good. All the challenges are part of your earthly journey, possessions and attachments. Since our Creator has blessed us with free will and choices, you've made a decision to live a certain way and sometimes setbacks occur. In fact, your faith in Divine Spirit must be strengthened in times of shortfall. Your setbacks are the result of an earthly ego, dependent on survival and an attachment to relationships which no longer work.

Twice I've experienced a real estate downfall as a homeowner. I've seen high unemployment among professionals working in fields such as technology, education and labor. Corporate restructurings create unemployment and small businesses can go under. I've seen several rocky marriages end in divorces due to challenges with finances, a lack of communication as well as other problems. I've observed three wars. It is easy to blame God during tough times. Learn to let go and release your addiction to materialism.

Cut loose from fearful or insecure relationships that don't include deep love. In several instances I've seen people cling to a failing marriage because of the children, finances and fear of the unknown. In this process, for most people God seems a million miles away.

Know full well God is right where you are. God is within, He isn't testing you. Just acknowledge and be aware of God's presence within. God loves you. Pray and meditate, then act on your prayers. As you pursue and strengthen your spiritual self, monitor and watch your steps. Avoid getting into the situations and circumstances that originally got you in hot water. God is your friend. He is with you all the time to lean on so you can be happy, joyful, kind and peaceful.

FAITH ~ PRAYER

Dear Lord,

I am thankful for the many miracles in
my life. I have faith in Divine Spirit (God),
available to all mankind through
awareness, recognition and just for the asking.

I have faith in God during tough times
to pull through, and at other times
that aren't tough, but merely routine.

Lord during tough times, I will pray,
meditate and ask you to strengthen
my faith in God to face all challenges with ease.
I know your guidance will help me
solve my problems, creating heaven on earth.

And, so it is!

PART IV
FREE WILL - DECISIONS

WALK THE TALK

FREE WILL - DECISIONS

I am surprised. Recently, I wrote a blog on ministering and serving. I mentioned the idea of carrying energy bars and canned food in your car for distribution to homeless people.

Today I went to a local ATM at my bank. Just as I was leaving the ATM, a woman in her forties with a pushcart, approached me and asked me for a quarter (25 cents). I didn't have any change with me. Instead, I had energy bars and a can of vegetable soup in my car. So, I offered her an energy bar and the soup. She took it. When she left with her pushcart, I noticed she lit a cigarette.

Maybe God was testing me to see if I'm walking my talk. Perhaps this woman changed her identity and came as a hungry individual as God's messenger sent to approach me. She was receptive to the food I gave her. This scenario was a great lesson for me in action. I didn't judge her in a critical way. She went on with her pushcart lighting her cigarette. God bless her.

In your walk of life, you're bound to face challenges. Use your

God-given mind and compassion for your fellow human being, regardless of their circumstances.

I mentioned earlier that I carry the phone numbers of local helpful organizations, such as homeless shelters, food banks and other groups for people who are economically challenged. The lists of phone numbers are next to my driver's car door storage area. Be prepared to give what you can and serve. You never know who might appear out of thin air ask for food or small change. I also keep a public bus schedule in my car. If someone is lost on a major boulevard, I can help them take the right bus to their destination, if they seek help. A nice way to help is to suggest calling a non-emergency number for sleeping and eating meals.

TAKE ACTION NOW

FREE WILL - DECISIONS

Do you ever wonder where all the time goes? Do you sometimes feel guilty about not doing something or not taking action? Every one of us are blessed and created with free will and the ability to make choices and decisions in our lives. God is available to every person in our the world.

You're an expression of God. You can be of any religion or spiritual belief system and God still resides within. So, what prevents you from not acting to fulfill your desires which will benefit yourself and others in so many ways?

Our learned human ego stops us. Whether it's through fear, procrastination, negligence, or complaining about not having enough time or enough resources to do what you want.

Develop confidence within yourself and then move forward. Prayer in conjunction with meditation is also helpful. A belief in God, Higher Power or Infinite Intelligence is incredibly helpful. Just do it. I recall needing to change jobs while working in the corporate world. I felt unsure of myself. Plus, I wasn't utilizing the power of prayer for myself back then. I kept asking my friends, "What would you do if you were in my circumstances?"

I became confused by all their "helpful answers", because I was in a state of information overload. Most of them were supportive. Now, I believe the greatest thing we can do is pray to find answers from within. Prayer is communicating with God and meditation is listening to God.

Finally, I decided to act based on my "gut feelings." Your gut feelings are your intuition. Trust your intuition, its God communicating His answers to you.

I meditated on my situation regarding my job. Soon, the right position appeared. When you seize the moment, you'll make a difference in your life. People around you will ask for guidance about how you did it and what made you so adventurous and successful.

Don't forget, you're in this world to learn and grow. We are ministers to each other and sharing your wisdom with others is a wonderful gift. There are so many decisions to make based on your circumstances: Should you take action or not? Which action? Health, prosperity, spiritual growth, love in your relationships, traveling, changing jobs, going into business, or simply being a seeker of the light. All require making gut decisions and coming from confidence and prayer.

USE GOD'S POWER AND SHINE

FREE WILL - DECISIONS

Are you falling behind in household projects? Is your "in basket" at work or your business piled up with "to-do lists?" Is your inbox clogged with emails? Do you procrastinate when it comes to visiting friends or doing volunteer work? Do you want to lose weight and feel healthy? How about paying a visit to family members out-of-state? The list goes on. We're taught early in life to take on responsibilities and accomplish things we deem important. If we don't complete goals at work or in life, the boss at work or our family members at home, or customers in our business will be dissatisfied or irritated.

Be aware God is always there for you, all the time, guiding you in your walk through life. He wants you to use your free will and decision-making abilities to fulfill your goals and your earthly expectations.

Several years ago, at the age of 65, I had a desire to do more "spiritual stuff". I was looking around to see what I could do to use my gifts to serve others, as well as earn income. First, I became ordained as a minister. Then, I started taking collected canned goods over to local shelters where homeless people sought refuge. I also donated clothing to help. Then I signed up to volunteer and visit with seniors at an assisted living center. I prayed and sang with the elderly. Then, I began officiating weddings and presiding over memorial services. No one told me or called me up and asked me to assist and volunteer or collect canned goods for the shelters.

The awareness I got to volunteer at an assisted living center and collect canned goods for the homeless came from within.

God works in each one of us to spread our energy, joy and enthusiasm and share it with others. Even when I worked in the corporate world as a Financial Analyst, I worked in an environment where I had to get the job done on time or I'd be counseled.

When you pray to improve your work or business, you use God's power from within and shine. You improve your family relationships by interacting with each other. God wants you to reach out. You can accomplish this by being aware of the Divine Spirit, which is infinite. Use it to harness your energy and creativity as you move forward to experience more joy in your relationships.

CHOOSE TO RELEASE NEGATIVITY

FREE WILL - DECISIONS

Our life journey is full of love, kindness, joy, happiness and adventure with a few bumps along the way. During a rough patch you may ask:

- "Why me? Why do I feel all this negativity?"
- Why I am angry, upset and irritated with some people?"
- "Why do I have ill feelings toward others?"
- "What's wrong with me?"
- "Why don't others like me?"

Questions like these can create heartache as you try to figure it all out. Learn to release negativity in your life. The following exercise may be helpful.

On a physical level, go in front of a mirror and take a good look at yourself. How do you look? Maybe a little self-reflection is in order. Perhaps you're not listening to God communicating to you from within. God has given you choices to make decisions in your life, which include listening to the guidance you receive.

A case in point is the heartbreak of divorce. Attorneys are in high demand by divorcing couples. But before seeking a divorce, the married couple was once loving and romantic. They had children and several years later, negativity developed. Learn to work out the negatives, forgive and move toward a positive healthy relationship again.

Better ways of rekindling the romance and falling in love again include praying together, communicating lovingly to resolve problems, and seeing God in each other's eyes.

Another form of negativity in family dynamics can happen among siblings. Feelings of jealousy, selfishness, power trips, a lack of caring and love, and out-of-control egos will cause negativity and distrust toward each other. The best way to mend this is to be loving; let go of the negative and forgive each other.

Even in business and work relationships there can be negativity between co-workers. When you understand the other, and recognize your co-workers' divinity in a loving way and work towards the benefit of everyone, positive feelings of kindness will return. When you see the Divine Spirit in others and send out positive energy and vibes, you build bridges. You make your world a better place at work and at home.

FREE WILL DECISIONS - PRAYER

Dear Lord,

Thank you God for giving me and everyone
free will to make decisions and
choices in our everyday walk of life.

Guide me to be in constant awareness of
my words and walk the talk to take action
which benefits myself and others.

Lord, help me release negativity and
get back to the positive realm
of creating heaven on earth.

And so it is!

PART V
PROSPERITY AND ABUNDANCE

ARE YOU BOMBARDED BY MATERIALISM?

PROSPERITY AND ABUNDANCE

How much "stuff" do you want to accumulate in your life? As we constantly experience the temptation of acquiring; be it a large bank balance, multiple cars, multiple homes, lots of furniture or high-tech toys, here are a few questions to ask yourself:

- Do I really need it?
- Am I driven to attract material things from my spiritual core?
- Do these things make me happy?
- Am I fulfilling God's plan for me on earth?
- Am I serving others or helping others?
- Am I just acquiring stuff to fulfill feelings of insecurity?
- Do I indirectly wanting to show off to others to be liked or gain respect?

These questions will help you think from the heart, communicate with God and seek out the best answers for you.

I grew up in India until I was 18 years old and came to America. I lived a humble lifestyle. I traveled in third class train compartments (these days they have two classes) because it was the most inexpensive way for students and people in the low economic strata to travel. What I've observed in America is, advertisers promote products rigorously and consumers fall for their claims. It's a great temptation and it results in spending little time and effort on your spiritual journey and growth. Maybe you attend weekly services and nothing else.

Most people lack awareness about including God in their everyday life. God is love. We get wrapped up working hard to earn an income or spending long hours running a business so we can contemplate how to buy more stuff.

Don't lose sight of God and stray from God's plan for you. Even in India, after several decades of economic and educational development, many residents are becoming more materialistic due to the influence of Western culture and technology. Our ego wants to experience the earthly things that are exciting, feel good, and provide a false sense of security and gratification. Don't lose your focus on your Divine Spirit. Be aware of why you're here on earth. You're here to spread the love of God, and to reach out, helping others and experience joy, peace and harmony.

PROSPERITY IS YOURS FOR ASKING

PROSPERITY AND ABUNDANCE

When we talk about prosperity, most people equate it with money and wealth. In fact, prosperity can be compared to succeeding in your health, relationships, spiritual growth, career growth and business growth, as well as your personal finances.

God's plan for you and me is to live and share joy, happiness, love, healing and help or support from those who need our help to improve themselves. Of course, many societies including ours have plenty of "haves" and "have-nots." We must work toward creating our own heaven on earth.

When you do the work to improve yourself while making your community better, you'll live joyfully, happily and peacefully. When you set boundaries on your hope and desire to improve, it's easy to neglect your God-given creativity. You may be faced with lack or, you may develop a selfish mindset toward what you already possess.

A good habit which will help you experience prosperity in all aspects of your daily life is prayer and meditation. Do you talk to God in the form of prayer? Yes, God listens. And, God communicates with you, when you're quiet or in meditation. Listen to the vibes, the inner communication.

Back in 1998, I decided to ride the Indian rails in all different directions across the subcontinent. At the same time I wanted to it in the form of a pilgrimage. I visited Hindu and Buddhist temples, Christian churches, Mosques, Gurdwara's (Sikh temples), etc. I also talked to Hindu Holy men, known as Sadhus. They're non-materialistic people who wander around practicing spirituality.

I talked to several Holy men on my ten-week pilgrimage, criss-crossing the Indian subcontinent, the country where I was raised. I left a contract job in the Los Angeles area with a year left, to take up the trip. Something inside my heart told me to go. India for a pilgrimage. My future wife, Denise encouraged me to take the trip. I was excited and didn't want to pass up the opportunity. So, prosperity comes in all forms. When I left at the age of 52, I was healthy and strong; I was able to handle sleeping on trains several nights at a time over a span of ten weeks. God blessed me in numerous ways, and I give thanks and praise for the experience.

FIND BALANCE IN OUR MATERIAL WORLD

PROSPERITY AND ABUNDANCE

The first 18 years of my life I lived in India. I was raised in a Christian family and attended a Methodist boarding school. All of my adult life I've lived in the United States. So, I grew up having less material "stuff" in India, and more stuff as I became an adult. I've found balancing materialism with my simple way of life is healthier, more peaceful and harmonious. We operate from free will and we make decisions using that gift in our everyday lives. We are blessed with these God-given attributes.

What is more challenging is when people become obsessed with possessions and get addicted year after year. Somehow many lose their spiritual life which is an awareness of love and caring for others.

Materialism makes many people behave in self-centered ways. But, some people also care for their loved ones and their neighbors as well as those who have nothing. The more materialistic we become, the less spiritual we become.

It becomes a way of keeping God at bay, leading to isolation and separation from people who need our help or support.

When you become God-centered, you pray and meditate for others and their well-being. Don't get me wrong about financially wealthy people. Some rich people care for others, but, homelessness and hunger still exist in our society. Imagine if a small group of multi-millionaires in each city pooled a little of their resources with the awareness and aim to eliminate homelessness together?

Pray for prosperity and abundance for the people in your community. Which means each person will be blessed by being able to use their skills, knowledge and faith. When they use their God-given attributes they better themselves and their experience of life.

The more you reach out to others; God will bless you in numerous unexpected ways. Learn to share and care for others. God or Divine Spirit wants all of us to care for others in our communities and beyond our nation who are in need. There is true joy, happiness and spiritual abundance when we reach out and help others.

PROSPERITY AND ABUNDANCE ~ PRAYER

Dear Lord,

Thank you, for giving me this wonderful day. I'm thankful for all the materials necessary to live every day, blessed with a prosperity mindset.

Guide me not toward addictions to materialism and commercialism, while losing sight of God and your blessings.

I pray and meditate for prosperity health, the ability to care for myself and my family.
I pray for those who are in need.
May they be blessed with helping hands providing the necessities to create heaven on earth.

And so, it is!

PART VI
RENEWAL AND THE POWER OF PRAYER

THE BENEFITS OF PRAYER AND MEDITATION

RENEWAL AND THE POWER OF PRAYER

When you quiet your mind and allow the chatter to diminish, there's a unique change which occurs in your mind and body. Take advantage of these quiet moments by dedicating a little time for prayer and meditation. Prayer is communicating with God and, meditation is listening to God. You can combine both into one.

Prayer is communicating your needs, wants and desires. Or, it can be simply sharing your appreciation and gratitude with God. It's about verbalizing and asking God for what you want to experience in your life such as healing from illness or better health, joy, prosperity, love, compassion, confidence, trust or anything else.

After sending out your prayer, listen to the still, small inner voice and act accordingly. Trust God's messages communicated through each one of us. Then apply them to your daily life so you experience true happiness.

To meditate, go to a private spot where there are no disturbances or distractions like electronics such as television, a phone ringing, conversation between family or friends or other disturbances, Simply quiet your mind. Never close your eyes while driving to meditate. When driving, always focus and stay present.

I tend to meditate at the gym in the spa, anywhere from five to ten minutes while the hot water bubbles up around me. Meditation is when you listen to Spirit from within while you cease the barrage of thoughts racing through your mind.

Your thoughts are constant as you think about what you must do, the problems you must solve, your job or thoughts about "acquiring things." Allow the quiet to happen like a soft, gentle silence washing over you. Open yourself to receiving thoughts and ideas which return to you from the vibrations, waves and thoughts you've sent out in prayer. This is the Law of Attraction at work.

You'll discover your own best way to form a habit of prayer and meditation all the time, throughout the day and evening. Through your faith in God, your beliefs and through prayer and meditation, you ask and become willing to receive. Then you will experience what you desire.

LISTEN TO OTHERS AND OFFER PRAYERS AND BLESSINGS

RENEWAL AND THE POWER OF PRAYER

I encourage my friends, neighbors, strangers, associates and online friends to pray for people seeking or asking for some kind of justice, consolation and comfort in their personal life or in their community. This provides peace, harmony and it's good for the soul. It also speaks to the importance of listening to your inner voice, which is the voice of God.

Currently, Americans are going through some soul-searching regarding the shooting death of young, unarmed African American men by police officers. Over the last few years there have been protests about this and many people deeply upset about the inherent unfairness and racism.

Law and order forces want to keep the peace. The two have repeatedly clashed. They can't relate to each other just by showing sheer power. If we try to understand each other and go within for answers, there is a good chance we can come up with solutions to resolve this highly sensitive issue.

When we see and hear people communicate and express their feelings and beliefs via their voice (or writings) about the way they feel; prayer and meditation will help serve as a spiritual mediator to create harmony, peace and bring comfort to others.

As I write this, our nation is involved helping Middle East nations in conflicts, such as Afghanistan, Israel/Gaza, Yemen and Syria. At the same time, we're going through a period of personal reflection and soul-searching regarding what's happening in our own backyard, including the loss of innocent lives and the mourning of those people who loved them.

Many Americans are shocked and find it difficult to understand. We have the people resources, technology and are willing to help in foreign conflicts. Yet somehow, we neglect to find solutions for problems in our own communities. God has blessed us with enormous intelligence, free will and choices for everyday living. We awaken our inner compassion only when there is a crisis in our communities, especially when an innocent loss of life occurs.

Through prayer and meditation, you can make a big difference in your community. Pray for leaders in the cities where this violence has occurred. Help leaders make the right decision to assist their residents with compassion and kindness so each person is treated respectfully while they express their disenchantment for the loss of life. Pray for those who have been hurt in these conflicts. We are all spiritual beings, having human experiences. Your faith in God through prayer and meditation, will bring harmony and healing to communities that are hurting.

YOUR PRAYERS GET RESULTS IN DIVINE TIME

RENEWAL AND THE POWER OF PRAYER

*D*o you ever get a sense and feel an urge to pray when your life becomes desperate and you need help fast? You might ask, "Why is this happening to me?" Remember, prayer is communicating with God and meditation is listening to God.

The process of prayer is about having faith in the infinite, something that's greater than yourself. When you send out your prayer requests, your vibrations and waves are received by others and communicated within yourself as well.

Pray as if you've already received what you want. For example, many people who are broke and who want help with money pray. After prayer, the best thing to do is release your prayer. Among friends, I've witnessed people after they pray. I see their outlook has changed from within. Their attitude is more positive and they become willing to receive from the giver.

I recall praying to raise funds to attend a spiritual convention. Some thoughts about how to make the money came to me like "officiate more weddings" or "seek out some temporary assignments." Then I let it go.

A few days later Denise said, "I have a birthday gift for you." Immediately I figured she bought me an electronic gadget, a new shirt or a gift card from Starbucks. Deep inside I wanted cash, so I could put it toward the convention in few months.

She told me, she reserved and paid for my accommodations for a full week so I could attend the convention. There was the answer to my prayer. I don't know how she read my mind.

Divine timing always comes at the right moment. Don't force your prayers and meditation with desperation. Believe in your prayer, don't just recite it or say it for the sake of saying it. After praying, release it to God. The more you pray, the more confident you'll become. I also discovered for myself, how to sprout creative ideas about how to make more money. This all springs from divine guidance. Ask for it and you'll receive it.

RENEWAL AND THE POWER OF PRAYER ~ PRAYER

Dear Lord,

Thank you, for this blessed day
and my gratitude to be thankful
for my life journey.

Lord, assist and guide me in my
awareness and constant renewal through
prayer and meditation every day,
to communicate with and listen to
you from within for answers to the
questions that will arise in my life.

I know the answers to all my
challenges are within. I'll listen gently and
take action to manifest results
creating heaven on earth.

And so it is!

PART VII
JOY AND GRATITUDE

PRAISE GOD FOR ANOTHER DAY

JOY AND GRATITUDE

I feel so blessed and grateful every day when I wake up in the morning after a good night's sleep. I thank God for giving me another day to live. Many of us take it for granted as each day goes by.

Look deep down in yourself and ask, "How can I be of service to others, and at the same time help myself?" When you think about helping others, most people get a feeling of deep joy and happiness down in their soul. When a friend and neighbor passed away suddenly with a heart attack just outside his home, I felt saddened. This happened several years ago. He had some health issues, but his death was sudden, unexpected, and it happened in broad daylight.

My friend and I used to go enjoy the sumptuous buffets at the Las Vegas casinos about once or twice a month. We'd discuss politics and international events. We also talked about our travel adventures, sports and much more. We even discussed God and religion. He was an intelligent, well-educated man, with a well-rounded knowledge of the world. He was fascinating to talk to and share ideas with. Suddenly and without warning, he died. I saw him early in the morning on a Saturday. By 11:00 am he'd dropped dead of a massive heart attack.

I'm sharing what happened because you never know what will happen to you on a day-to-day basis. No one knows how many days they have left. Since my friend passed away, I stopped reading obituaries in the newspaper.

Always look on the bright side of life. We have limited time on this earth and each of us should do our best to serve others and help them. In the process you're helping yourself.

You're so fortunate to have another day. Don't let anyone tell you it's a boring day or an unproductive day. God has given you and me this day. Be grateful with a full heart and soul. Be in the know; you're blessed to experience this day, regardless of how you choose to spend your waking hours. It's always beneficial to be kind, loving, and joyful toward yourself and others on this new day. Recognize God's love, spread it around and rejoice in your day.

TO EXPERIENCE JOY, SERVE OTHERS

JOY AND GRATITUDE

Many times I hear people say they're unhappy in their life. Or, they cannot seem to find happiness within themselves. The key is to get away from your negative thoughts and focus on bringing joy to others.

In our society we tend to say "me, me, and me." It's a form of selfishness and it can consume us from within.

When you feel insecure within yourself you may look for outward fulfillment. You may become obsessed with possessions, which leads to a central life theme of "more, more, more" where approval or you're blocked, unaware of your spirituality. As a person, God has given you all the attributes necessary to live with joy. When you are driven by ego it distance you from your spiritual awareness. When you ease your mind from wanting and release any obsessions, you can definitely shift your energy from inward to outward to help and care for others. Of course, chances are you'll help your immediate family and loved ones first.

Reaching out with kindness and a willingness to assist others will bring you a sense of joy and inner satisfaction. Your spirits will rise to new heights.

Even making simple phone calls to seniors living by themselves will make them feel elated when they know someone genuinely cares, and is reaching out. Remember, everyone eventually grows old. Everyone needs human interaction; especially lonely seniors who live alone or who've lost a spouse. I also suggest stopping by a senior center to visit the residents. Let the staff know you're there to greet and meet the seniors.

Offer a kind prayer and a warm smile to lonely people. It's great for the soul. There are others who need interaction and caring you can provide. Like in homeless shelters, some patients in hospitals have no relatives to visit them. When you reach out to others, somehow your own problems diminish. Your simple acts of kindness and love bring healing to both you and the other person. You're given the opportunity to look into yourself, and know you're blessed with good health, prosperity and a kind heart. It'll give you great joy to share your goodness and your smile with others, who genuinely need it.

TEACH CHILDREN GOD LOVES ALL PEOPLE

JOY AND GRATITUDE

God is love and, God loves all people. We live in a society with a variety of different races, cultural backgrounds, religions and upbringings. Parents and elders must teach children God loves all children and all people, regardless of how they look or their cultural or religious background. Lately, we've seen an increase in hate crimes against people of other races, some even resulting in loss of life. It is absolutely tragic.

When children are made aware of God's love for each one of us, and you spread that love to others in ways large and small, they'll get along better with others and their peers. They'll also lay a foundation of love for their friends and neighbors. It's all about bringing God or Divine Spirit into a child's awareness and into their life while applying it and sharing it with others.

My early experiences as a teenager in a Christian boarding school in India, taught me many valuable lessons about respecting students from other religious affiliations such as those raised as Hindus, Muslims, Buddhists, and of course fellow Christians. About 300 teen boys lived within the walls of the boarding school itself. There were a total of 4,000 students who attended classes from surrounding communities. Our boarding hostel Warden or Administrator encouraged the residents of the boarding school to respect each other's belief system and backgrounds. All the boys were encouraged to attend Sunday school, including the students with different belief system. It gave every student a sense of awareness to respect and honor our fellow students from different backgrounds. We were taught, God loves everyone.

When children are taught the love of God for everyone and they grow up to become adults, they won't simmer with hatred towards others, resulting in a more peaceful society. The notion of God's love should be taught early in childhood by parents and elders. When parents slide back and children go astray, problems start creeping up. This results in hate and discrimination, simply because some people look different and come from different backgrounds. The core of the young learning love and respect starts with the encouragement of parents and elders. I thank my boarding school Administrator who taught me about the love of God. Without their involvement and constant encouragement in my young life, I don't know how I would've turned out.

JOY AND GRATITUDE ~ PRAYER

Dear Lord,

Thank you for this wonderful and
blessed day. I pray and will take action to
help others in need with unconditional
kindness and compassion.

I will take initiative to teach children
and younger people that God loves all
people, regardless of who they are.

I will teach them with joy and gratitude,
to spread love toward others. As a result,
everyone will others create heaven on earth.

And so it is!

PART VIII
BLESSINGS

YOUR LIFE HAS A PURPOSE

BLESSINGS

*H*ere we are breathing, drinking, eating, working, learning, talking, laughing, crying, smiling, sleeping, creating, loving, caring, sharing, helping and more. You come into this life as a physical body having an experience of being human. Yet your physical life is temporary.

You are a miracle, created from the spirit of life, beyond human understanding. Our Creator has a purpose for each of us, including you. Your journey begins with the choices you make with your God-given free will as you pursue your voyage through life. Sometimes in our journey we take an ego ride or a trip. I define this as a power trip or a journey which is out of alignment with your heart, your mind and your body.

What can you do to return to a place of inner contentment? How do you return to assisting and supporting your loved ones, friends, neighbors and strangers locally as well as strangers who reside internationally? Many think living a "successful life" means growing abundant and prosperous with money, stashing it away for our future "retirement years." In the meantime, many neglect to care for themselves in the areas of health, time with our families, and self-reflection. We worry about the future, instead of doing the best we can as we go along in our journey of life. How about serving others in the capacity of volunteering? Give a little extra of yourself to those who need your support and time.

By offering to serve others you're being generous and noble. Plus, you get to experience inner contentment and joy. In the process the people who receive your help and support are thankful and you'll see a smile of gratitude on their face.

Choose to live your best life both physically and emotionally while making a difference. Immersing yourself in loving, committed relationships is another facet of life where we can always improve and become better men and women. Have you said "I love you" or "I appreciate you" to your spouse, your children or to a partner today? On this physical plane, many of us pick up unhealthy, unpleasant habits. Have you ever questioned why you eat unhealthy foods? Do you questioned why you become angry or impatient while in line at the grocery store or, on the highway?

When you ask questions and seek to know yourself better, you learn, grow and mature to enjoy a life of harmony and peace.

WE HAVE BLESSINGS AND LESSONS IN LIFE

BLESSINGS

On many occasions we're blessed with prosperity, like an excellent paying job or a thriving, successful business. At other times you may be blessed with a solid marriage relationship and plenty of friends. At other points in time you may have excellent health. It's not unusual to lose a job during periods of high unemployment. It's even possible to lose a business when a recession occurs in the economy. Marriage relationships can go up and down as well, due to the relationship dynamics. When things in your life seem to go hunky dory or "perfect," you probably experience a state of happiness. Moreover, many people pray to get rich and work hard at it. This sounds great. But, when, faced with challenges due to a downturn in the economy, a failing relationship or ill-health due to overweight or disease, many forget their countless blessings and blame God.

I recall going through a job search after losing my position as a Cost Engineer at an Engineering construction company due to an economic downturn. It was an upsetting and frustrating experience many years ago. I even blamed God temporarily. At the time,

I was also going through a divorce and wondered why I was dissatisfied with and unhappy in my marriage. Over the years we go through life wanting more. Maybe the materialistic environment we live in contributes to the desire for more.

As I mentioned in an earlier chapter, during a job layoff I volunteered at a church, handling telephone calls from people who were disturbed and experiencing tough times with their faith, their beliefs, their relationships, unemployment, problems with drugs, alcoholism, suicidal urges, dire financial problems, and more.

I realized I had some critical lessons to learn. Moreover, it came to my awareness how blessed I was to have excellent health and good friends around me in the midst of my problems. I learned from those people who were facing far greater hardships and challenges.

All the experiences we have as we go through life are lessons. God or Divine Spirit is still there, but you may be unaware of the blessings you still carry within, despite your personal challenge. It's easy to get lost, caught up with possessions, keeping your "standards" compared to others, instead of counting your blessings and giving gratitude to God.

GIVE THANKS TO GOD FOR YOUR FAMILY, FRIENDS AND PROSPERITY

BLESSINGS

*S*ome people have money and power. But it doesn't necessarily bring happiness and joy to their lives.

What brings us love, joy and happiness are family, friends and a sense or a feeling of prosperity in all facets of our lives. In many instances I've noticed when we constantly want and desire materialistic things and ego fulfillment, we tend to put God or Divine Spirit in the background of our lives.

Instead, give thanks to God by praying for the blessings of your family, your friends and for prosperity. The deep down sense of security and the feelings of love we experience from family and friends make us truly rich. For some hard to define reason, when we feel secure and comfortably prosperous, God the Spirit is recognized and not hidden away.

From time to time, I collect canned food for homeless people and deliver it to homeless shelters. People living in poverty come to the shelter to receive food to take home to their family. I look at their faces. They always seem happy to get a bag of food to take home. I pray these people can better their lives soon. The homeless people living in shelters receive help from contributions and donors. The shelter managers constantly ask for donations of money, to keep the doors of the shelter open. In Las Vegas, the city of lights; there is both extreme lack and extreme prosperity. Amongst the billion-dollar casinos and hotels with so much wealth that can be seen from the shelters, there is also homelessness. God will guide the angels to help and shelter the homeless. This guidance comes through our personal awareness and enlightenment from within.

I thank God with gratitude for what I have: A wonderful, loving wife, a nice home and food, friends, my sons and grandchildren and wonderful health. For me inner peace, harmony, and a sense of well-being are important. I encourage you to rejoice in what you have, be kind and caring toward each other. We are in this world to experience and create our own heaven on earth. I support you in your personal prayers and meditations, communicating with God. Listen to your inner voice from within and feel God's blessings.

ANGELS AMONG US

BLESSINGS

*I*n the midst of economic, social, spiritual and psychological challenges in our daily lives, there are angels among us who step forward to alleviate our suffering. These angels donate their time, financial resources, food and love. They're inspired by inner guidance, which is God in action. They're led spiritually from within. They see and observe the helpless and needy and are moved by their own inner spirit to alleviate suffering when they see it. This is their inner knowing and acknowledgement of people who need help and assistance. These incredible angels expect nothing in return. They give generously from the heart. Lately, I've noticed more homeless people begging for money on major street corners while I drive in Las Vegas, Nevada. Many of them stand with a cardboard sign which reads, "Homeless," "Hungry," or "God Bless."

When I can, I'll advise a homeless person to get some help from the agencies out there instead of begging on a street corner or in a supermarket parking lot. Several times I've seen homeless men in fast food restaurant parking lots. Some have mental and psychological problems and they neglect to seek care. Occasionally I see women asking for money in shopping center parking lots. In many states in America there are non-emergency phone numbers to seek help. For Las Vegas the number is 211. When the number is dialed, the person calling will get a visit from a help provider. Then, they'll be referred to the appropriate agencies for food, shelter, clothing or medical care. The helper will even come to meet a homeless person on the street corner where the person is standing. Some people are reluctant to seek help from the helping agencies, but they're there to help.

The angels among us are also known to volunteer at homeless shelters in the dining room or at their thrift stores. Angels are inspired and motivated to reach out to others. Everyone is a prospective angel. If you aren't currently participating or involved in helping the homeless and the hungry, why not jump in and reach out to them? It's wonderful for the soul and the receivers are always thankful. It will help your community as well.

BLESSINGS ~ PRAYER

Dear Lord,

Thank you for this blessed day and for my
purpose in this world, to journey
through life learning lessons along the way.

I will endeavor to be helpful to myself and
to others who are in need, or facing challenges.
I give gratitude for my
family, friends and for their wellbeing.

I pray and acknowledge the angels
among us and their blessings, who
reach out to others in times of challenge
for their wellbeing, creating heaven on earth.

And so it is!

PART IX
HAPPINESS

HEAVEN ON EARTH RIGHT NOW

HAPPINESS

This world we live in can be made a heaven. As the saying and the title of this book expresses, it's like "Heaven on Earth." We create our own heaven right here based on how we choose to live our lives and how we make decisions every day. Many of us are oriented to believe we can only experience heaven after our physical death and after judgement.

You don't have to wait until you die to experience heaven. Heaven can be right here where you are now. When you have thoughts and feelings of love, joy, happiness, compassion and caring, you're creating your own Heaven. When you help and love others, you're building heaven on earth. With so much disharmony in the world; with wars between nations due to power struggles, money and conquests, you can distance yourself from trauma and pain by living a joyful life.

During my life I've read about and observed wars in Korea, Vietnam, Northern Ireland, Iraq, Afghanistan, Bosnia and more. In some instances, war is a case of good over evil and political governance. Other times war is about what's good for a nation or what benefits it, in an attempt to acquire greater wealth. By loving and helping each other, we don't need to suffer through war. In fact, there would be no more need for war. The challenge is to put our leaders to work for the higher goals of peace and prosperity for all nations. If each leader from every nation makes an effort to bring about "Heaven on Earth" locally, everyone will succeed and get to experience joy, happiness and enlightenment.

As an individual, you can make a difference by focusing on love, joy, happiness, gratitude and compassion. Your self-reflection will give you the ability to reach out toward others and help where you can. Heaven on Earth is at hand right where you're living your life here on earth. Heaven isn't a mythical place up in the sky with the clouds. Pray to God or Divine Spirit for joy, happiness and your personal "Heaven on Earth" within yourself. Then share your love and joy with others.

ALLOW LIFE TO FLOURISH WITH HAPPINESS AND JOY

HAPPINESS

*Y*ou come into this world as a free spirit you were molded by the influence of parents, siblings, elders, teachers, religions, education, lifestyles, cultures, friends, peers, etc. You have a special uniqueness to share with the world. When combined with inspiration and motivation you're destined to succeed in life.

God, Higher Power or Divine Spirit, has created you with the free will and ability to determine how you choose to live your life. Of course, we all live in a human world with laws, regulations, restrictions, morality and man-made religious beliefs. You get to choose your experiences of work, family, friends and leisure so you live the life you want. As you keep moving forward in your everyday life, being responsible and accountable are in order. People who go "the wrong way" or "an evil way" have missed the mark in their life. God intended for you to live happily, joyfully and with compassion in your heart.

As you live your daily life, sometimes things don't go quite as planned. Interactions with others such as neighbors, friends, family members and strangers can create a sense of disconnect or disharmony. When you live from ego, you can get stuck, which prevents you from living freely. You're likely to hold on to grudges towards others rather than release them. This is a life lacking in peace and harmony. Learn to let go of grudges; they only cause pain. Forgive and forget by way of compassion. You're healthier when you live at peace with a kind heart. You become the master of your own destiny.

When you allow others into your life, open yourself up and accept them so they can open up to you. It's a give and take. Build trust in yourself and the people you allow into your life via interaction, friendship and mutual understanding.

Most of us are social animals. Like me, you probably aspire to share your life with the special ones you connect with and bring into your life. God is always there for you to acknowledge. Your sense of awareness allows God to be an integral part of your life. Treat God as a friend, and he'll treat you with love and kindness. God will never fail you. He wants you to be joyful, happy, loving, peaceful, compassionate and kind.

When you allow each day to unfold with an open mind and without self-criticism, you're bound to create ideas and plans which will make you happier and more content. Share with your family and friends the solutions or ideas you discover; provided they support you in a positive way. Remember, the Universe is vast, open and willing to assist and support you when you ask. Give thanks and appreciation to God for the fruits he has in store for you. Ask and believe as if you have already received. Keep your heart and mind open to experiences of prosperity, happiness, joy and compassion.

WE LIVE IN A SPIRITUAL WORLD BUFFETED BY THE PHYSICAL WORLD

HAPPINESS

As spiritual beings we are pure. I refer to a pureness of spirit where all is perfect. There's no need to fix or correct anything and your spirit is eternal. In the physical world as humans on planet earth, our experience is a temporary one. As humans, we're here on this earth to learn, to grow and to teach.

Have you ever noticed how you live on a daily basis? Most of us have man-made belief systems such as organized religion in which we've been raised. We obey certain rules, regulations and man-made laws governing our behavior toward our parents, siblings, grandparents, friends, strangers, communities and more. We're also measured in our society by how much money we earn. We become driven by our ego needs to excel in certain life directions. Of course, in the physical world, we are also judged by our appearance.

When I use the words "buffeted by the physical world" in this chapter heading, I mean we are pressured by concerns about the physical. For example, do you have a checking or savings account at a bank or credit union? Have you noticed how the rules and regulations about banking are applied to get each of us to "behave" and "act" in certain ways, adhering to the "money rules" in an organized setting? Sitting in a bank with a bank representative requires a calm, patient demeanor so the banker can provide you with the information you need.

First, you must qualify to open a bank account. The next time you rent a car while on vacation or a business trip, you'll notice the car rental agency first asks for your credit card and a driver's license. We are connected through a thin financial thread which protects the car rental agency, the bank's investments and the laws governing our streets and highways.

Of course as human beings, there are security authorities like the police and military for the safety and protection of everyone. The ego plays a critical role in human expressions of authority, such as power.

As human beings living in advanced and developing nations, we often live with certain fears. Fear of our fellow human beings, from other nations, cultures or tribes. I'm referring to fear in a world which is amassing nuclear weapons. Even though we don't intend to use them, if a bomb was dropped, we would all be in trouble facing challenges doing the simplest things like breathing, drinking water or cultivating food for sustenance.

In your walk as a human during this lifetime, you're endowed with free will and choice. Yet we all learn and are influenced by behaviors from others. In a way, we're tamed and trained.

We're here to experience love, joy, peace, happiness, harmony, kindness, compassion, gratitude, well-being, blessings, and love for God. So, your experience depends on how you use your free will, making decisions and enormous choices. Isn't it amazing, with one or two wrong decisions, you might also develop anger, hatred, selfishness, greed, neglect, rudeness, racism, bossiness, isolation, hunger, homelessness, fights and wars?

You were put on earth to gain the physical experience of life. This is your opportunity to learn, grow, get along and finally transition back to your spiritual being. What an adventurous journey!

SMILE! YOU ARE VIBRATING HAPPINESS

*U*se your God-given gift, your smile. Every person, brother or sister, can give the gift of a smile. When you smile, you send out vibrations from within and project them toward others: friends, loved ones, work associates, business clients, employees and even total strangers. A smile may sound simple, but, many people have difficulty smiling for several reasons. Maybe it's due to internal turmoil; life hasn't gone as expected. Perhaps you've had a misunderstanding with loved ones or you feel lonely. The list goes on. When you smile warmly, the world smiles back along with you. But, when you project serious or depressed feelings to the outside world, the feedback often is, "Who cares?"

Smiling is contagious. It comes from within and it propels positive energy. A smile is contagious and sends positive vibrations from you to others. Smiling is also healthy and good for the soul. The smile I'm referring to is a genuine one, not just baring your teeth "for the sake of smiling." That's a fake smile. Smiling is inner driven whether it's focused toward people or when observing the beauty of our world, like the majesty of ocean waves, a soft, purring kitten or glorious architecture. I smile at the gym when I pass by a fellow gym member. I don't smile merely for the sake of smiling. When I make eye contact, somehow my inner energy, which is God-driven, connects with the other person. Many people walk around unaware of the energy they're sharing. Next time you see someone, and they happen to share a smile, smile in return with genuine warmth and feeling before moving on.

If you have difficulty smiling even with your friends, practice smiling in front of a mirror. Practice at least three times a day. When I visit the gym usually five days a week, I reinforce my smile, opening my jaw fully while letting my teeth be exposed. While in the sauna I feel my cheeks actually pull back as I smile.

Smiling is good for your health. Spread your smile out to others and it will bring joy and a general feeling which uplifts your experience and the experience of the person you smile at. Use your God-given vibrations to shine as you smile. Go forth, spreading your smile and your magnetism; it's good for your well-being and the well beings of others.

HAPPINESS ~ PRAYER

Dear Lord,

Thank you for this blessed day. Guide me to
live fully in the present moment,
instead of living in the past or in the future.

I pray to remove stress, tension and excessive
materialism, in my everyday life. I will
be open to relaxation and happiness
for my wellbeing and for my family.

I live within my means, and I smile
every day sharing my contentment
with others. I allow happiness and joy
to come in my everyday life
creating heaven on earth.

And so it is!

PART X
PEACE AND HARMONY

SAY "I AM PEACEFUL AND HARMONIOUS" WHEN STRESSED

PEACE AND HARMONY

Recently I visited my family in Southern California. Most of the time when I go, I'll ride the commuter train, The Metro-Link, from Rancho Cucamonga to Union Station in Los Angeles to visit my long-time friend, Ravi. Many years ago I met him through work. The train ride takes about an hour and 15 minutes. On this last trip, to my surprise, the parking situation had changed at the Rancho Cucamonga train station. The last time I parked at the station, just three months before, parking was always free. But on this most recent stop, I learned the city had started charging a fee of $4.50 per day for parking, due to cutbacks in funding for parking maintenance. My train was scheduled to depart at 10:10 am headed for Los Angeles and I arrived in the parking lot by 9:30 am.

To my surprise, I noticed signs reading "Permit Parking Zone" throughout the parking lot. Hundreds of commuters had parked their cars with ID numbers on the dashboard of their cars. I was starting to feel restless and uneasy, since I didn't know about this sudden change in parking rules. I started looking for somebody, anybody, to ask about what was going on and how I could park for the day. I found a security guard and he told me the parking requirements were changed and it was no longer free. He said the city started charging for parking two months ago.

He also informed me I had 15 minutes to get a parking permit from the machine, place it on my dashboard and park before the train arrived to pick up passengers on their way to Los Angeles. He also advised me to look carefully at the screen on the machine because it was facing the sun, during the morning hours.

Yes, it was difficult to read the instructions on the screen due to the sun's glare on the glass. I managed to buy the parking permit with my debit card. The machine wouldn't accept cash. All during this time, I kept saying to myself, "I am peaceful, I am harmonious."

To make matters even less convenient, the train ticket machine wasn't working. By now, the train was less than ten minutes away.

I kept repeating to myself, "I am peaceful, I am harmonious." Luckily the same security guard was standing at the station. I told him the problem with the ticket machine. He told me to buy my ticket on the train and pay the conductor. Of course, when I stepped on, the train was less than 25 percent full, because it was after rush hour. I finally was able to relax after the "hustle bustle" learning the new parking permit system, dealing with the glare of the sun and the malfunctioning train ticket vending machine. What a relief it was to get on the train and enjoy the ride.

"I am peaceful. I am harmonious."

LET GO AND LET GOD

PEACE AND HARMONY

*L*ife isn't always joyful, happy, loving, prosperous, peaceful or harmonious as we'd like it to be. We're on a journey and we're growing through our learning experiences as we go along. Problems and conflicts arise in our family relationships. You may have problems with work associates, business partners, with children and grandchildren, spouses' relationships, money problems and more. Sometimes you don't have control over the circumstances and situations. Problems and challenges can become enormous and you may find yourself unable to cope.

Some people drink alcohol, take drugs, or even become violent toward their spouse or children. You may try to rationalize or psycho-analyze why these prolonged problems nag at you. You may feel like you can't cut loose or escape them. The more they linger, the more life becomes stressful and tense. Some people even experience a nervous breakdown.

We live in a culture which encourages a level of independence and individuality. It's common to hear a young child say, "I'll do it by myself." Or they might say, "I don't need any help." To a degree, this is encouraged.

While I was a volunteer phone on the crisis line at church, many callers asked me how they should solve their problems. They gave up on solving their own problems and often found themselves cornered. For some, their problems seemed enormous. I did my best to help.

The best thing to do when confronted with lingering problems isn't to try to take control but to also Let Go and Let God.

Many people cling to unhealthy, controlling habits and behaviors. They have a tough time letting go. God or Divine Spirit is far greater than we are. Learn to trust God who exists right there within each of us. He has the power to release all our problems and free us from bondage. Learn to communicate with God through prayer and listen to His answers. God communicates quietly through each one of us. Having faith and trust in God, will help alleviate your deepest problems when you let go and let God do the magic. You don't need a complicated prayer. Just ask using simple words and believe. Your request and belief will make a difference.

YOU ARE NOT GOING TO HELL

PEACE AND HARMONY

If you're interested in knowing about "Hell," do a little Google research into how it became known and its origin. Look at it this way: God loves you, regardless of how much you've messed up in your life. Of course, you're responsible and accountable for your actions.

We have laws and regulations in our society which are in place to keep our homes and our communities' safe and functioning normally. When many people do something "bad" they've been taught they'll go to Hell for their actions. This is what many religious belief systems teach.

It doesn't matter how messed up you may think you are, God still loves us. Every other human being may leave you, but, God will never leave you. It's all about your belief, your faith and your acceptance of God. You're always loved and you're not going to Hell. But thinking you are can create your own Hell on earth.

When God loves us so much, how can we possibly be harmed or punished? God is always love. Always. We are a miracle called life.

Give thanks and gratitude for your existence. The Divine Spirit has put you on earth for a unique purpose. To love God, is to love yourself and to love others. You don't have to live in fear. Fear is man-made, and God balances it with love for everyone.

All the current and past wars are man-made as a result of ego and a struggle for power. When you use your God-given free will and make choices in your life for your good and for the good of others, you'll naturally experience joy and a sense of enlightenment.

God has given you the wisdom and knowledge to choose your lifestyle without harming others. When you heal your vices, mistakes, or miss the mark in your walk of life, simply ask for God's forgiveness sincerely and you're forgiven.

To assist you in experiencing peace and harmony, reach deep into your heart and release love so you can share it with others. This means do good for others. Have you:

- Considered feeding the hungry in your community?
- Talked with a police officer and thanked them for keeping you safe?
- Helped an elderly person by taking them to a doctor appointment or by buying them groceries?

Hell on earth happens when we use our free will to go astray and deviate from God's plan.

PEACE AND HARMONY ~ PRAYER

Dear Lord,

I am grateful for this peaceful, blessed day. I let go and let God with all my problems and challenges.

I will seek to find answers within me through prayer and meditation. I will have faith in miracles which have the power to heal us from disharmony.

Lord, guide me in my awareness to believe in myself as I peacefully solve problem within. In turn I will strengthen the bonds with my family and friends, sharing peace and harmony, creating heaven on earth.

And so it is!

PART XI
FORGIVENESS

FORGIVENESS IS GREAT FOR THE SOUL

FORGIVENESS

If you feel any animosity or anger toward others due to "their faults," mistakes or sins against you, make the choice to forgive them as quickly as possible. It can be difficult to forgive especially when crimes which cause broken hearts, ill feelings and sadness are committed.

Did you know the word "sin" in ancient Greek means "to miss the mark?" When you miss the mark, you have free will to correct it and get back on the right path. For some reason, the word "sin" is largely misunderstood even by most clergy. Over the centuries, the word "sin" has come to mean something scary, especially among many believers. It often keeps people of every faith who believe in God in a constant state of fear. You can simply correct your course by doing the right thing.

Many people live their life with buried anger, resentment and constant reminders of other people's crime or action against you. The best way to resolve things and gain closure is to make a final decision to forgive and let it go.

The first step in forgiveness is to forgive yourself and then, forgive others. Pray for God to release you from any feelings you have of guilt or remorse. Then, release others who need forgiveness, too.

When forgiveness happens, you'll experience a sudden feeling of ease, lightness, harmony, peace and understanding within yourself. You free yourself by forgiving yourself and others who may have hurt you.

Forgiveness is a wonderful virtue. Experience peace, joy and finally achieve closure as a result of your decision to forgive.

HAVE YOU FORGIVEN YOURSELF?

FORGIVENESS

We go through life and encounter plenty of ups and downs along our way. What you may not realize is the Divine Spirit or God, always resides within you. I realize I've said it already on these pages, but I hope you'll truly embrace it.

Since everyone makes mistakes, errors and occasionally causes ill feelings to ourselves and others, it's time to reflect and forgive yourself first. Then, go ahead and forgive others as I suggested in the last chapter.

When you don't allow your God-center within to function freely, and instead you let ego take over your attitude so you project it towards oneself and others, you live with constant guilt and anger. God wants you to be peaceful and experience joy and happiness. When you don't forgive, there is no peace, harmony or joy. Getting even to "settle the score" makes it even harder to achieve reconciliation.

I recall in my early career I held a position as a Cost Coordinator. I tried to prove I was right and an older gentleman co-worker was wrong about some reporting information. He was about 30 years older than me.

Later that day, I felt guilty and went to his office and apologized for my arrogant behavior.

Back then, the idea of Divine Spirit within was alien to my thinking. I didn't know God is within and was also within my co-worker. My senior co-worker apologized too, saying he felt sorry about the incident. I instigated the issue, but he accepted my apology and we made peace with each other. Afterward, I learned to have greater respect for him and for others.

When you forgive yourself, God's presence will vibrate throughout your body as you communicate a heartfelt apology to another person.

Acknowledging God's presence with love makes us feel more peaceful and makes it easier to treat others with respect. People will extend greater respect to you as they sense a change within you. As a result, they'll change and become more peaceful and harmonious. This isn't a complicated formula, its simple forgiveness.

Our communities and our nation both use forgiveness so everyone can move forward with a better understanding of each other. Allow God's love to flow through you and you're bound to eliminate obstacles and see your circumstances more clearly. You'll get better results in life when you forgive yourself and forgive others.

RELEASE THOSE OLD GRUDGES

FORGIVENESS

*H*ow many times have you gone through your daily walk of life and held grudges, dislikes, hate, a lack of concern, unkindness and more toward other people? True, we're all flawed, imperfect human beings. We all get hurt feelings and each of us makes mistakes.

The longer you hold grudges against others, the more unhappy you'll become. Your unhappiness will prolong a state of anger, sadness, and disharmony. There is a disconnect and misalignment from your spirituality and your relationships with others.

As spiritual beings living in a human shell, we all need to balance the two and be more like God. You were made in God's image and likeness. When you're far removed from this, unhappiness is the result until you're back in sync with Spirit again.

God has a plan for you in this life. To see God in others, learn to forgive when there is hate, anger or unkindness.

Over the years I've seen families with siblings, in-laws and married couples who've developed grudges with each other.

Here's a case in point: While working as a financial Credit Counselor helping clients manage their personal finances and credit, at times there was a great deal of animosity with spouses blaming each other for their money problems. I also witnessed parents who gave their college-age children credit cards. The children don't understand the responsibility involved with having a credit card. They would spend lavishly and create enormous debt. Then, the parents would blame their college-age children. The blame game would spiral endlessly downward.

I've also seen one brother pitted against another brother due to some financial deal gone wrong. The two found it impossible to forgive each other.

Forgiveness must come from the heart and soul. At least forgive yourself for your mistakes and for being irresponsible. You made a mistake. Just get back on the right track.

Say a prayer of forgiveness. Meditate and self-reflect on forgiving yourself. I've met people who've written a letter of forgiveness to the other person. Usually they never mail it, choosing to keep it to themselves. That's fine. The purpose of a letter of forgiveness is to express a desire to forgive and move on with a clear conscience and heart.

When you let go of grudges and forgive, you make all your family relationships more peaceful, joyful and harmonious.

HOW DIVERSITY TAUGHT ME TOLERANCE

FORGIVENESS

I grew up in India until the age of 18 when I came to the United States. I was born into an Indian Protestant Christian family. Both my parents were Christian. In India there are several religions among the 1.3-billion people who call India home. My family and I lived among Hindus, Muslims, Sikhs, Buddhists, Christians and Jains in the major metropolitan area of Mumbai (formerly Bombay).

I mentioned in a previous chapter, I attended a Methodist boarding school, located in Hyderabad, South India. In boarding school and in my classes, there were also Hindu, Muslim and Buddhist students. This experience helped me learn to respect all religious beliefs; even though the people of India are 80 percent Hindu, 14 percent Muslim and only two percent each Christian and Sikhs.

The diversity of beliefs and religions made me curious. I wanted to study the various religions to understand them better. I lived with my family in communities where a great deal of spiritual diversity existed. I played with children from different backgrounds and went to school with them.

At 18 after high school graduation, I came to the USA and joined my father. Later my mother, sister and brother migrated to America. I'm proud to have grown up in such a diverse background in different Indian communities. The experience taught me tolerance and understanding. This eventually paved the path to me becoming a non-denominational Interfaith Minister as an adult.

In the USA I've lived in different cities. I started in Washington DC for a couple years. I spent 35 years in Southern California and I've lived in Las Vegas, Nevada with Denise since November, 2001. I've experienced the racial diversity of each city. My family and I have lived in communities with African-Americans, Hispanics, Whites and Asians and learned to live peacefully with everyone.

Coming to America also empowered me to seek out and experience churches of different Christian denominations including Catholic, Presbyterian, and Methodist. I've learned about and come to appreciate other beliefs which have added to my understanding, tolerance and belief systems. I've attended both Unitarian and Meta-Physical churches. Each provided me with extensive devotional and meditational experiences and a tolerance toward all belief systems.

Living at peace around people of different belief systems and races provides a sense of respect and appreciation for others.

God works through each one of us and you're an expression of God within. When you live a life of tolerance, understanding and caring, you experience joy, harmony, generosity, understanding and compassion toward others. When you're open to others and respect who they are, you can appreciate them for their uniqueness.

FORGIVENESS ~ PRAYER

Dear Lord,

Thank you for my wellbeing and for this blessed
day. Lord, I forgive myself for missing
the mark in circumstances with others,
my mistakes, my wrongdoings, my errors
and my misunderstandings with others.

Lord, assist me in my awareness. Release
me from holding grudge against myself
and others. I instantly forgive others and
myself, as many times as necessary,
even if it means hundreds of times.

I will learn from my mistakes to clear
my conscience, creating heaven on earth.

And so it is!

FORGIVENESS ~ PRAYER

PART XII
CARING AND SERVING

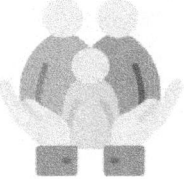

WE ARE MINISTERS AND MESSENGERS

CARING AND SERVING

A while back a young woman came up to me in the parking lot of a local grocery store, and asked me for food. I wasn't even there to buy groceries. I went to return DVD movies.

I gave her instructions on where food is served at the Las Vegas Rescue Mission, Catholic Charities and at the Salvation Army. This was on a Saturday at about 5:15 pm. Since she had a car, I told her the general area where the shelters and food kitchens were located and where she could get a hot meal. She continued asking other customers in the parking lot for food. I doubt if she collected any food while asking people in the parking lot during the time I was there.

I even told her to call 211, a statewide non-emergency, 24-hour service number. It provides access to a number of community-wide services and agencies.

Just to experiment and see how the 2-1-1 number works, I called the number locally in Las Vegas. I was the first caller of the day at 9:00 AM. The woman instructed me to visit the website at –

http://www.nevada211.communityos.org, to check out all the services available. Food is free, and some groups want recipients to fill out paperwork to receive it. Others don't require any paperwork. I read about the services offered on the website and came away feeling grateful to God we have such resources available in our community.

Next, I made copies of the phone number and address of food banks to distribute to people who are pandering for food or money. I keep some copies in my car and carry a list of phone numbers for shelters as well.

We are all ministers and messengers tasked with being kind and helpful to others. There is a need in every community. Some people are unaware of what's available to them. Others only want a quick buck. I believe in treating the needy with kindness and empathy. Show them different ways to care for themselves. High school and college students should also know about 2-1-1 services and helpful people to call. Or, you can volunteer to call on behalf of someone in need at the moment. I encourage you to look at these services in your own state and community. We're ministers to serve those who are in need and who want help.

HOW DOES GOD USE YOU TO SERVE YOUR COMMUNITY?

CARING AND SERVING

*M*ost of us get caught up in our own self-fulfillment. It's easy to become isolated from our community, as the addiction to acquiring more gets out of hand. Some people volunteer their time to serve others. Their kindness goes beyond the norm as they ask, "How can God use me to serve my community?"

When considering service from a spiritual perspective, go deep into your soul and ask how you can best serve God. Whether you call it God, Spirit, the Universe, Higher Power or another name, it's all the same.

Do you listen to your inner voice when it calls you to serve others? Sometimes it's a matter of listening to the guidance you receive from Spirit within. When you act, your compassion, understanding, love, concern and sharing will be revealed. Prayer and meditation will help you go deep within as you ask God for guidance. God works through each of us. Your free will can help you make good choices as you face numerous life decisions.

It's not just the homeless, the hungry or the street wanderers who need help. You may discover family members, friends, co-workers, neighbors, communities, and online friends need help as well. Learn what is needed by interacting with people with whom you connect. Issues where you may be able to help including dealing with stress, tension, sadness, misunderstandings, small financial help, providing company, listening, being a support system, being there in times of bereavement, going walking to improve your health, sharing knowledge, sharing food, collecting food and other possibilities. You can even provide transportation to doctor appointments and the grocery store.

Serving from your heart center in alignment with your connection with the Divine will give you a sense fulfillment in your daily life. Responding to a God-centered calling to help others will help you experience feelings of harmony and wellbeing toward yourself and the people you help.

There is a great reward when you help others. This journey isn't necessarily tied to expectations of compensation or pride in what you provide. You'll be humbled as you see humanity. Take action springing from God within and show your love and caring.

God is always within. To help others, simply acknowledge and act on God's light within.

ARE YOUR SPIRITUAL BELIEFS SHORT ON ACTION AND DEED?

CARING AND SERVING

Your manmade religion has a purpose. It provides a source of devotion, faith and love, to help yourself and others. It provides a community where you can love God, experience unity and adhere to societal laws and guidelines. Belief in religion or spirituality serves as a personal foundation in your life through your understanding of God which was handed down by your ancestors, often stretching back centuries.

I enjoy taking the time to observe different belief systems in action and how they apply to our everyday lives. Your faith is paramount to your spiritual life and what you do. The tenets of these beliefs can be summarized as: love, kindness, compassion, helping others by being God in action, unity, peace, respect for others, respect for laws, doing the right thing without harming others, reaching out, understanding and tolerance.

Do you apply the tenets of your faith or belief system to create your own Heaven on Earth? Or, do you fall short of joy, happiness and comfort?

Consider the great challenges our nation faces along with other countries? Immigration has become a crucial issue with children being transported to the US border from Central America by the thousands. Refugees from Syria and other war-torn, destitute countries risk life and limb to reach Europe with only the clothes on their back. The issue of immigration reform in America always seems to stagnate in Congress. People go hungry in our own communities as homelessness, families in disarray, financial distress due to job loss, business setbacks and illness go unaddressed.

Since, our religious belief systems are meant to serve as an anchor, we can all do better by reaching out, taking action and noticing positive changes in our lives and in the lives of others when we help. Applying the tenets of your belief system to your daily life must be part of your faith. God never intended for us to pray in a vacuum and do nothing in the outer world.

Move forward to act and help others. Become a positive testimony and example of God in action. Start a daily practice of prayer and meditation. Pray for our leaders to make the right decisions in our country and in your community. Share your gratitude, blessings and miracles large and small with others. Forgive those who've hurt you in the past and reach out with love.

CARING AND SERVING ~ PRAYER

Dear Lord,

Thank you for this blessed day. I pray to
be more thoughtful, caring and sensitive
to others in need in my community, in
our region and around the world.

Assist me to serve them in times of
hardships and serve them with love,
so I'm able to better their lives,
creating heaven on earth.

And so it is!

PART XIII
YOUR PHYSICAL SELF

IS YOUR BODY A TEMPLE?

YOUR PHYSICAL SELF

In 1998 I went back to visit India, the country of my birth, for ten weeks. After over three decades in America I was used to eating cheese burgers, hot dogs and pork with plenty of cola to wash it all down. I also used to pour sugar in my tea or coffee to make it sweeter. I exercise regularly but I ate unhealthy food. After returning to America from India, the first thing I wanted after leaving Customs and the airport was a couple Whoppers from Burger King® and a large cola. I told my then-girlfriend Denise, I missed hamburgers. In fact, once back on US soil; I ate Whoppers every day for two weeks after my trip to India where I ate no beef or pork. I felt deprived of my American favorites while I was away.

In India most people don't eat beef or pork for religious reasons. Hindus respect and worship cows and Muslims don't eat pork because they consider it unclean.

When I first arrived in the United States from India I'd never eaten beef or pork. As I settled in America, I started eating both and I drank plenty of cola most of my adult life.

In 2002, doctors told me I had high cholesterol and suggested I cut back on red meat and exercise more often. I followed up on what the doctor told me and brought my cholesterol level down. In 2006, after seeing the documentary, "Fast Food Nation" I stopped eating beef and pork. Instead I now eat turkey, chicken, fish, eggs and nuts. Plus plenty of vegetables and fruits.

When I say your body is a temple I'm referring to the respect and honor with which you treat your body. What happens when you feel unhealthy? Just because meat is plentiful and available everywhere in America, many common foods we enjoy regularly are unhealthy. Is eating unhealthy foods respecting and honoring your body?

For many years I drank Diet Pepsi. I added sugar to my coffee and tea so it "tasted better." But people pay a high price when they're diagnosed with diabetes or heart disease as they grow older.

In our land of plenty many people indulge in bad food without questioning their choices. It's easy to get caught up in the American idea we must eat meat at every meal. We also ignore our junk food choices for convenience and neglect our health.

Americans and people from other countries have grown addicted to cola and other soft drinks to the point they can't eat a meal at a restaurant or fast food joint without it.

Is this respecting and honoring your body?

Just a little food for thought.

I AM HEALTHY AND PROSPEROUS

YOUR PHYSICAL SELF

In our society, many people associate prosperity with:

- Money or currency
- A stake in the stock market
- A big bank account
- Owning a large business
- A large house or fancy cars

Of course, it's partially true, but it's not 100 percent correct. This entire book has been about exploring prosperity on a more holistic level. Of course we must pay our way, pay our bills and save, enjoy good health and excellent relationships.

The way you live will return you back to your original beingness; driven by the power of the Infinite or God which sustains you. The ego within plays a role as well.

Most people realize money is important to make a daily living as well as to save for the future. As excessive materialism flourishes, our health often faces problems as a result.

As I've lived in America throughout my adult years, I've observed people who continuously eat and drink unhealthy foods.

In the last few years there's been a trend with bacon in everything. You can order donuts and ice cream sundaes topped with bacon. Almost every chicken sandwich features a couple slices of bacon. It's bacon this and bacon that. So a hamburger that's already unhealthy is combined with unhealthy cheese and topped with unhealthy bacon.

The fatty strips have been incorporated in most menu items at fast food joints and cafes. Do you eat only for the sake of flavor?

The owners of fast food establishments only care about revenue and profit. Do they care about their customers' health? They're waiting for something to happen, which seems to be a reaction by customers who want to stop the widespread addiction to unhealthy foods. Add to all the fatty foods the sugar-laden sodas most people consume throughout the day.

Unless we all become more aware regarding our health and our choices when we eat, nothing will change what restaurants offer. It seems money is the only motivator for profit-driven food establishments. If people get sick and die eating unhealthy food, restaurant owners might change their marketing. I believe only consumers can bring a change by changing their habits.

God has blessed us with free will. We're also blessed with the knowledge of how we can choose and consume healthy foods.

If we refuse to listen to God's calling for better health, as individuals and as a society we'll pay the price. Many will leave this world prematurely as a result, gone from their loved ones before their time should've been up.

I've shared the concept of money prosperity and relationship prosperity. Without healthy relationships, especially with family and close friends, we can be isolated, lonely and unhappy. Our affiliation with employers, co-workers, business vendors and other professionals is a part of our holistic prosperity, too. Eating healthy foods and engaging in moderate, consistent exercise is the way to create health prosperity.

*E*veryone has need to belong. God communicates through each one of us encouraging us to create healthy relationships and live a life of peace and harmony with family, friends and strangers.

Learn to be thankful to God for the prosperity you experience on your journey. Our life is precious and we should treat it with love and respect.

When you affirm the I AM which is God, you affirm your spirit and subconscious mind, appreciating the fact you've already received your own benefits of holistic prosperity to live a joyful, happy life. A sense of inner contentment is sure to follow.

ACCEPT WHO YOU ARE AS GOD CREATED YOU

YOUR PHYSICAL SELF

*D*o you want to emulate and copy the bright stars, entertainers and athletes you see on TV and online? Remember, God has special plans for you and what the Almighty wants you to do and become. Many people wish they could be like a famous singer, dancer, actor or musician, while pursuing their daily life, either working at a job or running a business.

Over the years, I've developed a love for singing, while working in the corporate world, at non-profits and as a substitute teacher. On my own, I'll sing or whistle the lyrics of well-known songs from America or abroad. I sing out of sheer joy and pleasure. And the act of singing feels good in my heart.

Over the years, I developed an interest in Mexican Mariachi music. I like the song "Besame Mucho" which in English means "Kiss Me More". Dean Martin used to sing Besame Mucho, but, he sang it in English. I used to just listen to the song by Mariachi Vargas de Ticalitlan as there are no English lyrics that align with the Spanish.

So, I gradually learned and memorized the words to Besame Mucho in Spanish. Sometimes I'll sing it while washing dishes or driving on the freeway. The melody somehow touches my soul. Appreciating talented stars and singing a few tunes is different from becoming obsessed and wanting to be like them. There is a difference and I accept it.

I admire some popular Mariachi vocalists, and have memorized some of the lyrics to their songs. All these singers contribute to our pleasure as we listen to their wonderful songs.

You need not have a perfect voice to sing. Singing brings joy and music to the soul. The famous singers are superstars in their field. Most have perfected their voice over the years.

Remember, God made you a unique person in this world. You're contributing to yourself and others, with your knowledge and experience, in your chosen profession or business endeavors. It's wonderful to admire and appreciate others, who contribute to your enjoyment by singing. Just don't compare yourself to a superstar. Simply be you.

Another vocalist I enjoy singing along to is Nat King Cole. I especially enjoy his classic "Mona Lisa." I learned the lyrics to the song and mesmerized my wife on Valentine's Day recently when I serenaded her singing, "Mona Lisa." She listened with tears in her eyes. I still sing "Mona Lisa" while washing dishes or at the gym, with my headset plugged in.

My admiration also goes to Perry Como, who sang, "Home for the Holidays." In 2015 before Christmas, I memorized the song, and sang it in front of three different business networking groups in Las Vegas. It gave me great joy and the roomful of small business owners burst into appreciative applause. Como, a wonderful vocalist, brought joy to millions in his heyday.

Singing the tunes you resonate with will bring a special joy to your soul, reduce stress and depression and improve your well-being. As you sing you actually minister to yourself as well as to others.

I feel inspired and joyful when I sing spiritual and devotional songs. One hymn I used to sing while volunteering at a senior assisted living center, and while simply "puttering around" is, "How Great Thou Art." Elvis Presley recorded the song and sold millions of records worldwide. I admire Elvis for putting his faith on his sleeve and singing a spiritual hymn. The vibration and devotion it carries offers praise to God.

Singing is a way to please our hearts and please God. You are a living, breathing miracle. Be the unique person God created you to be, without comparing yourself to the superstars. Bring joy to your heart to others and to God by singing with joy and gusto.

YOUR PHYSICAL SELF ~ PRAYER

Dear God,

Thank you for this wonderful adventurous
life journey. I am grateful for my
excellent health, emotional interaction
and prosperity.

I accept the way I am, just as God created
me. Lord, grant me the inner knowingness
to use all my talents, my expression
and my creativity to live a life of joy,
happiness and inner contentment,
creating heaven on earth.

And so it is!

ABOUT THE AUTHOR

Reverend Ernest D Martin

"A World Traveler and Observer of Life"

Reverend Ernie Martin, known as "The Reverend of Love," is an ordained minister. He received his MS Degree in Business Organizational Management. He is happily married, has two grown sons and three grandchildren. Prior to ordination, Reverend Ernie worked in the non-profit sector as a Job Coach for adults with disabilities, a Volunteer Coordinator, and as a Financial / Credit counselor, he's also worked in Las Vegas high schools as a Guest Teacher. He volunteered as a phone Lay Minister at the former Crystal Cathedral in Orange County, California.

Before retirement, Martin worked in a Fortune 500 Aerospace company as a Project Financial Analyst prior dedicating himself to supporting non-profit organizations and schools.

ABOUT THE AUTHOR

Ernie was born and raised in a Christian family in India. His family lived among a myriad of people from different religious groups including Hindus, Muslims, fellow Christians, Buddhists and Sikhs. He came to America at age 18 in 1964. Reverend Ernie has learned extensively about other religions and belief systems through his studies over the years. In America as an adult, he actively attended several churches including Catholic, Protestant, Methodist, Unitarian and Meta-physical.

He was ordained by the Universal Life Church Monastery in January 2011. Reverend Ernie has volunteered at senior living centers conducting non-denominational services involving prayers, singing and sharing experiences.

He has also volunteered for and supported the Las Vegas Rescue Mission and other charitable organizations. Rev. Ernie serves as an independent Wedding Officiant, a Celebrant, and is a Guest Teacher in Las Vegas area public schools.

Ernie and his wife Denise live in Las Vegas, Nevada.

∼

E-Mail: heavenonearth787@gmail.com
Website: www.reverniemartin.com

Facebook: https://www.facebook.com/erniemartin
Twitter: https://twitter.com/reverniemartin

848 N. Rainbow Blvd. #297 Las Vegas, NV 89107

COMING SOON

Please visit the website for news about
How to Create Your Own Heaven on Earth:
A Spirit-Centered Journey for Everyday Living
Book II [COMING 2021].

E-Mail: heavenonearth787@gmail.com
Website: www.reverniemartin.com

www.ingramcontent.com/pod-product-compliance
Lightning Source LLC
Chambersburg PA
CBHW070640050426
42451CB00008B/237